# Fear and
# Other
# Uninvited
# Guests

## By the Author

*Fear and Other Uninvited Guests*

*The Dance of Connection*

*The Mother Dance*

*Life Preservers*

*The Dance of Deception*

*The Dance of Intimacy*

*The Dance of Anger*

*Women in Therapy*

*Franny B. Kranny, There's a Bird in Your Hair!*
(with Susan Goldhor)

*What's So Terrible About Swallowing an Appleseed?*
(with Susan Goldhor)

# Fear and Other Uninvited Guests

Tackling the Anxiety, Fear, and Shame
That Keep Us from
Optimal Living and Loving

## Harriet Lerner, Ph.D.

HarperCollins*Publishers*

HarperCollins books may be purchased for educational, business, or sales promotional use. For information, please write: Special Markets Department, HarperCollins Publishers Inc., 10 East 53rd Street, New York, NY 10022.

FIRST EDITION

*Designed by Joseph Rutt*

Printed on acid-free paper

Library of Congress Cataloging-in-Publication Data
Lerner, Harriet Goldhor.
    Fear and other univited guests : tackling the anxiety, fear, and shame
that keep us from optimal living and loving / Harriet Lerner.—1st ed.
      p.  cm.
  ISBN 0-06-008157-0
  1. Fear.   2. Anxiety.   3. Shame.   4. Self-actualization (Psychology).
I. Title.
BF575.F2L47   2004
152.4'6—dc22                                2004042893

04 05 06 07 08 ❖/RRD 10 9 8 7 6 5 4 3 2 1

In memory of my mother,
Rose Goldhor

# Contents

ACKNOWLEDGMENTS     xi

CHAPTER 1     Why Can't a Person Be More Like a Cat?     1

CHAPTER 2     The Fear of Rejection: A One-Day Cure     14

CHAPTER 3     Terrified? You Have to Keep Showing Up!     27

CHAPTER 4     In Praise of Anxiety: How Fear and
Trembling Keep You Safe     39

CHAPTER 5     The Trouble with Anxiety:
How It Wreaks Havoc on
Your Brain and Self-Esteem     53

CHAPTER 6     Why We Fear Change     73

CHAPTER 7     Your Anxious Workplace:
Staying Calm and Clearheaded
in a Crazy Environment     92

CHAPTER 8     The Secret Power of Shame     117

CHAPTER 9    The Fear of the Mirror:
             Anxiety and Shame About Your Looks—
             and Being Looked At                         141

CHAPTER 10   When Things Fall Apart:
             Facing Illness and Suffering                171

CHAPTER 11   Courage in the Face of Fear                 196

EPILOGUE:    Everyone Freaks Out                         221

NOTES                                                    225

INDEX                                                    231

# Acknowledgments

For careful editing, invaluable conversation, hand-holding, com-
miseration, encouragement, and generosity of spirit during the
writing of this book, I thank my dear friends Jeffrey Ann Goudie,
Marcia Cebulska, Emily Kofron, Joanie Shoemaker, Stephanie von
Hirschberg, Marianne Ault-Riché, Tom Averill, and Stephanie
Bryson.

For these same gifts, my boundless love and gratitude go to my
husband Steve Lerner, my sons, Matt Lerner and Ben Lerner, and
my niece Amy Hofer. Members of our wonderful, ever-expanding
family have been described by Matt as being at once "the greatest
intellects and the silliest clowns." No slouches here in the writ-
ing/editing department, either, I might add.

My manager, agent, and close friend Jo-Lynne Worley brought
her unwavering competence, intelligence, and commitment to this
project, as she does to all that she undertakes. For over a decade, she
has facilitated my work beyond words. New on board is Marian
Sandmaier, whom I discovered through *The Psychotherapy Networker,*

and who proved to be a superb, creative editor and long-distance support. For assorted help, thanks to Hazel Browne, Ellen Safier, Jen Hofer, Yarrow Dunham, and Mary Fulton. I am also grateful to Mary Ann Clifft, who contributed to this book by meticulously compiling the index.

Thanks (yet again) to the people at HarperCollins who have published my books for almost two decades. It's a rare author who happily chooses to stay for so long with one publisher. I'm particularly indebted to Gail Winston, for spare and splendid editing, and to Christine Walsh, Cathy D. Hemming, Susan Weinberg, and the many other people at Harper whose labors have kept me in print. Thanks also go to Will Staehle for his inventiveness in the book jacket department.

Thanks to my enthusiastic readers, to therapy clients who have shared conversations with me since the start of my career, and to the countless unnamed individuals to whom I owe intellectual and emotional debts. And big hugs to Alice Lieberman and Susan Kraus for their spirited, energetic friendship and for welcoming me so generously to my new home in Lawrence, Kansas, while this book was in progress. Boundless love and appreciation also go to the remarkable Vonda Lohness, who has kept me organized and afloat for ten years before heading off to a new life in Clearwater, Florida, thankfully, after the completion of this book.

My mother, Rose Goldhor, died in Cambridge, Massachusetts, during the writing of this book. Rose was the most loving and intrepid of mothers to me and my sister, Susan, and a warm, openhearted, generous grandmother to Matt and Ben. She is always with me. This book is dedicated to her.

Fear and
Other
Uninvited
Guests

# CHAPTER I

# Why Can't a Person Be More Like a Cat?

"Fear stops me from doing so many things," a neighbor confided when I mentioned the subject of this book. Then, without further ado, she launched into a description of her coworker Carmen, a woman who exuded such a deep sense of calm, joy, and peacefulness that everyone wanted to be around her. "Carmen *never* feels fear or other negative emotions. She's *always* in the flow of the present moment. She *really* lives each day to the fullest." My neighbor paused to catch her breath, then exclaimed: "I would do *anything* to be like Carmen!"

She spoke so earnestly, her voice ringing with italics, that I restrained myself from suggesting that maybe Carmen had multiple personalities and that one of her alters might be sitting mute in some corner having wall-to-wall panic attacks. But I did tell her this: The only being I have ever known who was entirely free of fear and always "in the flow" was my cat, Felix. When Felix was alive, I aspired to be like him, much as my neighbor aspired to be like Carmen. I could relate.

## FELIX, MY ROLE MODEL

Felix was my little Buddhist, my role model for mindful living. He demonstrated a healthy fight-or-flight response when threatened, but he only felt fear when fear was due. He became anxious and agitated when forced into a carrying cage, because he knew very well it meant a car ride to the vet. But he didn't let fear, worry, and rumination spoil an otherwise perfectly good day.

By contrast, I recall my own human experience anticipating my first allergy shot as a child. For a good week before the actual appointment, I freaked myself out with fearful imaginings, all of them having to do with long needles and terrible pain. My mother, who had certain Key Phrases to Live By, informed me that "a coward dies a thousand deaths; a brave man dies but once." She learned this aphorism from her younger brother when he went off to fight in World War II.

I personally found no comfort in her words. What sense did they make to a nine-year-old? I wasn't brave, I wasn't a man, and why was my mother bringing death into the conversation? When I was older and had developed the capacity for abstract thinking, I understood the lesson she was trying to convey. In essence, my mother was encouraging me to be more like Felix.

Felix lived in the moment. When he played, he played. When he ate, he ate. When he had sex, he had sex, utterly unencumbered by fear, shame, or guilt. Once "fixed" (the downside of being a pet), he settled immediately into a perfect acceptance of his situation. "Wherever you go, there you are," was the motto I believe he lived by.

This capacity to inhabit the moment granted Felix a kind of profound self-acceptance. When he licked his fur, he didn't worry about whether he was doing the job well enough, or whether he was taking too long to lick down all his hair, or whether certain of his body parts weren't all that attractive and perhaps shouldn't be displayed to my dinner guests. Nor did he dissipate his energy with anxious thoughts such as: "What's wrong with me that I don't make more fruitful and creative use of my time?"

Because Felix didn't live a fear-driven life, he was able to operate from his essential Felixness. When he wanted connection, he would jump on my lap without stopping to wonder whether I might find him too needy and dependent (especially for a cat). With equal aplomb, he would jump off my lap and saunter out of the room when he felt like it, never worrying that I might take his departure personally and feel really hurt. I could go on, but you get the picture.

A sociobiologist friend tells me that I have an idealized notion of Felix's inner emotional and spiritual life, but I disagree. I'm not saying that all cats are like Felix. I've seen my share of traumatized felines who cower or scratch when strangers approach. But I observed Felix almost daily for more than ten years before he keeled over dead one afternoon on our back porch. I'm convinced that it simply wasn't in his nature to get bogged down in fear and shame.

## Face It, You're Human

Of course, Felix didn't have it all. If he missed out on the miseries of being human, he also missed out on some uniquely human pleasures, from reading a riveting novel to falling in love. One might debate whether it is preferable to be a cat or a person, but why get into it? If you are reading this now, you are not a cat and never will be. So along with the good days, you're going to experience the entire range of painful emotions that make us human.

This means that you'll wake up at three in the morning searching your breasts for lumps. You'll worry that your daughter has dropped out of her drug treatment program (again), that your partner is getting bored with you, that you'll end up a bag lady if you leave your job, that your memory is getting more porous with each passing day, and that possibly you're going crazy.

You can make your own list. No one is immune to the grip of anxiety, fear, and shame—the "big three" that muck up our lives. These are the uninvited guests. When tragedy or hardship hits, they may become our constant companions.

## SIX EASY STEPS TO CONQUERING FEAR AND ACHIEVING BLISS?

I bristle at feverishly inspirational books that make large and silly promises. Break free from fear and you'll soar like an eagle, reverse the aging process, and attract a bevy of wildly sexy and appreciative lovers. I recently eyeballed a new self-help guide that states: "Bliss is available to anyone at any time, no matter how difficult life may be." When I read such statements, I am prone to entertaining mean-spirited thoughts, such as hoping that the author is dealt some unfathomable loss that will serve as a test case of his or her bliss theory. Since I am really a very nice person, these are but passing uncharitable fantasies. Still, I believe it is arrogant and deeply dishonest to tell people that they can transform their own reality, no matter how dreadful their circumstances, with the acquisition of a few new skills and a brighter attitude.

Of course, each of us can move in the direction of experiencing less fear and more calmness, love, and peace. This is a worthwhile and entirely possible venture. Meditation, therapy, friendship, creative pursuits, exercise, yoga, gardening, authentic conversation, reading, and listening to music are but a few of the paths we can take to become more whole and centered and, in the process, lessen fear's grip. With practice, we can also change our habitual ways of thinking. We can't stop bad things from happening, but we can stop our relentless focus on how things were or how we want them to be, and develop a deeper appreciation for what we have now. There is no quick fix, however, when it comes to managing fear and suffering in our lives, or even for coping with the simple stresses of ordinary life.

## DECODING FEAR

Fear is not something to be conquered or eliminated—or even tackled, for that matter. Instead, we may need to pay close attention to its message. Most of us experience fear as a kind of stop sign or flashing red light that warns: "Danger! Do not enter!" But we may need to decode that signal and consider what it's trying to convey. What is the actual nature of the danger? Is it past or present, real or imagined? Are we feeling anxious because we are boldly charting new territory, or because we're about to do something stupid?

Sometimes we feel a stab of fear or a wave of anxiety because our unconscious is warning us that we're truly off track. Perhaps we shouldn't send that angry e-mail or buy that adorable "fixer upper" house. Maybe we shouldn't rush into a particular job, conversation, trip, marriage, or divorce. In such cases, fear can operate as a wise protector, one we need to honor and respect.

Yet if fear was always a legitimate warning signal, we might never show up for a doctor's appointment, speak up when we feel passionate about something, or leave a dead-end relationship. There are times when we need to push past our dread and resolve—with our hearts pounding in our chests—to act.

At still other times, we may need to identify the actual sources of fear—past or present—that may be obscured from our view. For example, the anxiety that washes over you when you contemplate confronting your spouse may mask an underlying, ancient terror of speaking up to your father when you were a child. Clarifying these deeper sources of anxiety may help you to talk straightforwardly with your partner. Fear is a message—sometimes helpful, sometimes not—but often conveying critical information about our beliefs, our needs, and our relationship to the world around us.

There is one final kind of fear we need to decode—the fear we don't feel at all (at least, not consciously). When we can't fully face our anxiety and clarify its sources, we tend to act it out instead—attacking a colleague, nagging our child for the twelfth time, or working all weekend on a project that was good enough on Friday afternoon—all the while convincing ourselves that these responses are totally rational and warranted.

When anxiety is chronically high it leads to more serious outcomes such as greed, bigotry, scapegoating, violence, and other forms of cruelty. In these anxious times, on both the personal and political fronts, ideas are embraced and decisions are made not on the basis of clear thinking that considers both history and the future, but rather on the basis of hearts filled with fear. We owe it to ourselves and others to learn how to recognize behaviors that reflect and escalate anxiety—and to manage our own anxiety so it doesn't get played out in hurtful ways.

## AFRAID AND ALIVE

We may believe that anxiety and fear don't concern us because we avoid experiencing them. We may keep the scope of our lives narrow and familiar, opting for sameness and safety. We may not even know that we are scared of success, failure, rejection, criticism, conflict, competition, intimacy, or adventure, because we rarely test the limits of our competence and creativity. We avoid anxiety by avoiding risk and change. Our challenge: To be willing to become *more* anxious, via embracing new situations and stepping more fully into our lives.

Some people (James Bond comes to mind) escape anxiety and fear because they are disconnected from their emotional lives. I confess to envying such people—they seem to stride so intrepidly through life's difficulties—but I'm also aware that such "courage" comes at a cost. Feelings are a package deal, and you can't avoid or deny the painful ones without also forfeiting part of your humanity. If you are never fearful, you may also have trouble feeling compassion, deep curiosity, or joy. Fear may not be fun, but it signals that we are fully alive.

## Fear That Connects, Fear That Isolates

On September 11 fear barreled straight into the heart of our national psyche. Within a few months of the terrorist attacks I had filled two big cardboard boxes. One was stuffed with magazine and newspaper articles addressing how citizens could cope with their heightened feelings of vulnerability to terrorism. The other box was filled with literature on how psychotherapists could help them manage their fear. Much of the advice, I realized, was applicable to coping with all the scary events and possibilities that life plunks in our path. For example:

1.  Talk! Talk! Talk!

2.  Go for the facts. Anxiety escalates and fantasies flourish in the absence of information.

3.  Be reasonably vigilant. Don't be ashamed if there are certain risks you choose to avoid.

4.  Don't go overboard on numbers 1–3.

5.  Steer clear of activities that just rev you up (for example, turn off the TV).

6.  Seek out activities that calm you down (for example, after you switch off the TV, take a brisk walk or do some yoga stretches).

7.  Keep perspective. Terrible things happen, and it is still possible to move forward with love and hope.

8.  Connect! Connect! Connect!

September 11 certainly wasn't the first time that many Americans, especially members of disenfranchised groups, had felt themselves to be potential targets of hatred and brutality. Yet the attacks on 9/11 were obviously not just another fear-producing event. The nature and scope of the devastation, along with its moment-by-moment documentation on television, the subsequent wars and their aftermath, and repeated White House predictions of imminent terrorist attacks produced a level of national dread that is unprecedented.

At the same time, this "national diagnosis" of anxiety and grief, in the words of Dr. Rachel Naomi Remen, engendered an experience of deeply felt connection, a sense that we were all in it together. Both in New York City and around the country, citizens coped with the catastrophe collectively, and reported feeling more connected to friends, family, and even strangers. Those who suffered losses knew that millions of people were feeling for them. Simply say "September 11" and nearly every American understands—as do people throughout the world. The enormity of the experience has been acknowledged everywhere.

By contrast, when something terrible happens to you as an individual, your fears may go unspoken, unheard, or even disbelieved.

Even close friends and family members may not want to hear your experience, or they may communicate that they don't want to hear *all* of it. They may behave as though the anxiety-producing event is not really happening or has never happened, or that maybe it is happening but you are *way* overreacting. In response, you may begin to feel isolated and disconnected. You may feel shame about your honest fear and suffering and for failing to pull yourself up by your bootstraps and march forward in the ever-resolute, can-do American Way. You may wonder why you were "chosen" for tragedy or whether you did something wrong to bring it about. These sorts of private crises are especially apt to trigger not only fear and anxiety, but also other "uninvited guests" such as shame, loneliness, and depression.

While an individual crisis is different from a tragedy of devastating magnitude, fear is a universal human experience that can serve to bring us together if we learn to respond to it wisely. Sooner or later the universe sends everybody a crash course in vulnerability and a lesson in how much we need people. We can't avoid fear and suffering, but we can choose to encounter it in ways that will help us to feel connected and whole again. Fear can teach us how to keep participating in that most basic human activity of giving and receiving help.

## ABOUT THIS BOOK

I was inspired to write about fear because it operates as such a powerful force in everyone's life, whether it holds us back in love and work—or propels us toward disaster. Indeed, anxiety, fear, and shame (which we'll get to shortly) are the culprits behind almost all the problems for which people seek help—or fail to—including problems with anger, intimacy, and self-esteem. While a comprehensive list of all human problems would be a long list indeed, what *fuels* human unhappiness in both the personal and political realm can be boiled down to these three key emotions—anxiety, fear, and shame. Or, more accurately, it's the nonproductive ways we *react* to these uninvited guests that creates and perpetuates most of our misery. Perhaps nothing is more important than understanding how these emotions affect us and how to manage ourselves when we are in their grip.

Since I am no stranger to unwanted emotions, I'll be sharing personal stories in the chapters that follow, along with examples gathered from my work as a psychologist and therapist. What this book *won't* do is lay out a new, seventeen-day plan to help you stop panicking. Nor is it comprehensive in scope. There is already a wealth of books and online guides to mastering the whole range of anxiety-related problems, including phobias, panic disorders, and post-traumatic stress responses. There are programs, with or without medication, to help people master debilitating fears of specific activities, from flying to crossing bridges to stepping out of their homes. There is also a vast literature on meditation, imaging, and relaxation techniques to help people control their breathing and muscle tension as well as change habitually negative thinking patterns. I won't repeat these worthy efforts.

This book will look fear full in the face, challenging readers to consider this difficult emotion as both obstacle and friend. I view anxiety and fear as necessary, and necessarily complex, emotions that can squelch our hopes and prod us to take healthy risks, threaten our relationships and help keep them intact, consign us to predictability and remind us that we are fearfully, pulsingly alive.

I hope to provoke, advise, and inspire you to use fear to guide you in a positive direction, and to manage anxiety wisely and well, at least a good part of the time. We can also learn courage, so that our fear does not stop us from speaking, acting, and living authentically. In the words of the late poet Audre Lorde, "When I dare to be powerful, to use my strength in the service of my vision, then it becomes less and less important whether I am afraid." And when fear temporarily gets the upper hand, I hope this book will help you to feel more compassionate toward yourself and others. Finally, I hope to make you laugh along the way, because, as my friend Jennifer Berman says, without humor nothing is funny.

## Facing Shame

Shame will get a large share of attention in this book. Many common fears—the fear of rejection, intimacy, social situations, or speaking in public—are about shame. At bedrock is the fear of being seen as essentially flawed, inadequate, and unworthy of being loved.

Shame is so painful that no one talks personally about it or wants to "go there." When was the last time you discussed your shame at the dinner table? Shame is the least-talked-about emotion because people are ashamed of their shame—whether it's shame about your body, your teenager, or how you chew your food. Shame steers people into a life of silence, inactivity, lying and hiding. Or, to avoid feeling shame, we may flip shame into contempt, arrogance, or displays of one-upmanship. We can learn to do better than that, to face shame and not let it stop us from being our best selves.

## Fear vs. Anxiety

Most of us make some distinction between fear and anxiety. Sometimes it's merely a matter of linguistics. We say we have a fear *of* something (flying, aging) and anxiety *about* something (flying, aging). Sometimes we distinguish the two by our bodily experience. I'm sure you're aware that the neurobiology of fear is different from the neurobiology of anxiety. The sudden rearrangement of your guts when an intruder holds a knife to your back (fear), is different from the mild nausea, dizziness, and butterflies in your stomach as you're about to make a difficult phone call (anxiety). Anxiety is also the word of choice to describe lingering apprehension, or a chronic sense of worry or tension, the sources of which may be totally unclear.

But the notion that "fear" always connotes something bigger and stronger than "anxiety" breaks down in real-life experience. You can have a short-lived fear response to the bee buzzing around your face, and you can wake up at three in the morning awash in anxiety that won't let you get back to sleep. When the distinction between "anxiety" and "fear" isn't critical to the discussion at hand, I use just one of these words as the umbrella term. Anxiety, apprehension, fear, terror—however you name it, what matters is how you cope.

In everyday conversation, we use the language of emotions that we're comfortable with and that fits our psychological complexion. I've worked with clients who don't report feeling anxious or afraid. "I'm incredibly stressed out . . ." is their language of choice. "Stressed" is the codeword for "totally freaked out" for people who are allergic to identifying and sharing their own vulnerability. Or, at the other linguistic extreme, a woman in therapy tells me that she feels "sheer terror" at the thought that her daughter's wedding dress will not fit her properly. I know her well enough to translate "sheer terror" into "really, really, worried."

Whatever your emotional vocabulary, no one signs up for anxiety, fear, and shame, or for any difficult, uncomfortable emotion. But we can't avoid these feelings, either. I am convinced that the more we can look these uninvited guests in the eye, with patience and curiosity, and the more we learn to spot their wisdom as well as their mischief, the less grip they will have on us. Only when we experience our emotions as both potential stumbling blocks and wise guides—not either/or—can we begin to live more fully in the present and move into the future with courage, clarity, humor, and hope.

## A Road Map

Here's a brief road map of the territory ahead:

Chapters 2 and 3 include a bit of "fear lite," to demonstrate that facing the fear "of" something (rejection and public speaking) need not always be a somber and heavy matter. Here we'll see the hidden advantages of having your dreaded fears actually happen. Chapters 4 and 5 explain how fear keeps us alive and well, and also how it wreaks havoc on every aspect of our functioning. Chapter 6 reveals why we fear change, new learning, and adventure—and for good reason. Chapter 7 illustrates how anxiety is not just a characteristic of individuals but also an invisible force that flows through all human systems. I use the workplace to spell out the signs and symptoms of an anxious system, and to show how we can manage our personal anxiety more productively.

Chapters 8, 9, and 10 include a more in-depth look at the wrenching ways that the universe sends us lessons in fear and shame, for example, having a body that looks all "wrong" or breaks down altogether; the shame we feel about another family member, or about our flawed, imperfect self. Chapter 11 is about the hidden faces of courage and the never-ending challenge to speak and act even when we are afraid, and have internalized the shaming messages of others. Saving the best for last, the brief epilogue reveals the six secret, simple, specific steps you can take to banish unwanted anxiety, fear, and shame from your life forever. Just kidding, but yes, that would be nice.

# CHAPTER 2

# The Fear of Rejection:

## *A One-Day Cure*

Cured in a day? It happened like this:

I was surprised to get a call from Frank, a former client who now lived in Tulsa, Oklahoma. His work was bringing him back to Kansas for a two-day seminar, and he wanted to know if I would meet with him. I hadn't seen Frank since he and his wife, Ann, terminated marital therapy with me many years earlier. They appeared to be doing well, but Frank told me that shortly after they moved to Tulsa, Ann ended their marriage. Frank was devastated at the time, but he reported that he was now doing fine—"except for one thing."

"What's the problem?" I asked.

"Maybe I was traumatized by the divorce," Frank replied, "but ever since Ann left me, I've been phobic about rejection." He went on to explain that he hadn't dated since his marriage ended two years earlier. He was drawn to a woman at work named Liz, but the mere thought of asking her out paralyzed him.

Although Frank used the words "phobic" and "traumatized," he was neither of these things. He was merely terrified. I suggested that he see a therapist closer to home, but Frank made clear that he had no interest in embarking on a whole new therapy process. He simply wanted to pick my brain for one session about how he might solve this specific problem.

I knew that Frank was a roll-up-your-sleeves, fix-it sort of guy, so it didn't surprise me that he hoped for a quick solution. Since I more typically work with people slowly and over time, I was uncertain how much help I could provide in a single session. But I had recently attended a workshop conducted by Cloe Madanes, a psychotherapist acclaimed for her innovative transformational strategies. I recalled one particular intervention that Madanes had described for a man whose problem was quite similar to Frank's. I had a strong intuition that this directive would be perfect. At worst, it would do no harm.

## Change: How Badly Do You Want It?

I was about to give Frank an extremely challenging assignment, so I wanted to know if his motor was running for change.

"On a scale of 1 to 10, how motivated are you to solve your problem?" I asked him. I explained that "1" meant that he'd like to ask Liz out, but, in truth, he didn't have much energy to work on the problem. A "10" meant that he would do anything—dangle from the Golden Gate Bridge—if he knew it would accomplish his goal.

"I'm a 10," Frank replied without hesitation.

"Good," I responded, "because what I'm about to suggest won't be easy. On the plus side, it requires only one day of work. If you carry out this assignment to the letter, it will cure your problem."

"Shoot," Frank said.

## Standing at the Bottom of the Escalator

Frank had defined his problem as a fear of rejection. "The real problem," I told him, "is that you don't have *enough* experience with rejection." To solve his problem, Frank needed to accumulate rejections. His assignment, if he chose to accept it, was to rack up seventy-five rejections in one day.

He was to proceed as follows: The day before his seminar in Kansas City, he was to go to the Plaza, a major shopping mall and tourist magnet. Starting at Latte Land, a popular coffee shop with a relaxed, informal atmosphere, he was to approach several women (one at a time, of course), and say: "Hi. My name is Frank. I hope you don't think I'm rude, but I'm wondering if you would like to have coffee with me." After getting his feet wet, he was to walk down the street and station himself at the foot of a department store's escalator. As women came down the escalator, he was to repeat his lines: "Hi. My name is Frank. I hope you don't think I'm rude, but I'm wondering if you would like to have coffee with me."

He was not to veer from this script. He was to keep an accurate record of his accumulated rejections and stop only when he reached seventy-five. Obviously, I said, he should exercise good judgment and discretion so that he wouldn't be reported to the store management for harassment. He could rotate escalators, as the store had several, and move to the bottom of an escalator in a different store, if necessary. I asked him to call me after he returned to Tulsa to report the results.

Frank was intrigued by the idea that he needed to pile up rejections to make up for his lack of experience. The directive struck him as both daunting and absurd, but his motivation was sky-high. He also was spurred on by his confidence in me, and by my assurance that if he completed the assignment, he would be able to ask

Liz for a date. It probably helped a bit that Kansas City was no longer his hometown.

"I can do anything for one day," he said.

## Rejection Boot Camp

When Frank called me a few weeks after returning to Tulsa, he was full of good cheer. "I failed," he blithely told me.

At first, he had followed my instructions to the letter. At Latte Land he accumulated three rejections. Then a woman accepted his offer, which made Frank realize that stacking up seventy-five rejections might take longer than he had initially imagined. At his next location, he collected five more rejections off the bat. Then, once again, he ran into the problem of several women saying "yes." Rising to the challenge, Frank became more strategic about scoping out women who would be highly likely to reject him—those wearing wedding rings or herding small cranky children, for example.

It wasn't long before Frank's motivation dropped sharply— "from a 10 to a 2," he admitted. As his will faltered and his irritation rose, he suddenly spotted a stunningly gorgeous woman stepping onto the escalator. A good six inches taller than Frank, the woman wore an ultra-fashionable silver minidress and was, Frank said, "steely-looking and ice-cold in her demeanor." Here was the last woman in the world he would ever approach or be interested in—and he was quite certain that the feeling was mutual. "I didn't think I could get up the nerve to approach her," Frank said. "But I decided to give myself fifteen bonus points if I did."

As she glided down the moving staircase toward him, Frank felt increasingly ridiculous. He recognized that even with the bonus points he was planning to grant himself, he would still need to collect more than thirty additional rejections. The very thought made him tired. Then a lightbulb went off in his head. With a loud sigh of relief, he moved to a more secluded part of the store, took out his cell phone, and called Liz.

When he got her answering machine, he didn't miss a beat. "Hi, this is Frank from work," he said. "I hope you don't think I'm rude, but I'm wondering if we could have coffee together when I get back to Tulsa."

"It was so *easy*," Frank told me, wonder edging his voice. "Calling Liz was a million times easier than asking that ice queen for coffee and completing the assignment. The only reason I was standing there to begin with, feeling like a total idiot, was to ask Liz out." Frank reported that he spent the rest of his afternoon sightseeing, shopping, and thoroughly enjoying himself.

As for Liz? It turned out that she was already involved with someone and declined the coffee date. But several days later Frank approached a woman he sometimes chatted with in his neighborhood—"a dog person like me"—and asked her out. She accepted, and they've been dating ever since. "And you know what?" Frank told me with a laugh. "I did *not* say, 'Hi. My name is Frank. I hope you don't think I'm rude, but I'm wondering if you would like to have coffee with me.' "

## Into the Belly of the Beast

By following my directive, Frank plunged into the very center of his fear. I didn't advise him to slowly desensitize himself by moving toward the dreaded situation in carefully measured increments. Nor did I encourage him to undergo another round of therapy to explore the psychological underpinnings of his fear, such as low self-regard or unacknowledged rage at his ex-wife. Instead, when Frank reported his crippling fear of rejection, I sent him off to accumulate rejections at record-breaking speed.

Why was this assignment successful? When Frank's problem was reframed as "a lack of experience with rejection," failure became impossible. Every rejection constituted a resounding success, while each acceptance ("Sure, I'd love to have coffee with you") obstructed progress. Moreover, merely starting the assignment required Frank to ask a woman on a date, which he initially claimed he could not do. Also, his assigned task was so thoroughly staged—he had to stand in a certain place and repeat certain lines—that he had no room to become anxious about his approach or berate himself for saying something "uncool."

Most importantly, the assignment put Frank squarely in charge of his own symptom. Rather than being a passive victim of his greatest fear—rejection—he became actively engaged in making rejection happen. And Frank took the directive seriously because he respected and trusted my judgment. Though he stood alone at the bottom of the escalator, he knew I was in his corner.

## Should *You* Stand at the Bottom of the Escalator?

As I shared Frank's story in a seminar for social workers, a student inquired: "Would you give that directive to *anybody* who wanted to get past their fear of rejection?"

Of course not. I knew Frank's vulnerabilities and strengths from my previous work with him in marital therapy. His motivation to move forward was very strong, and he specifically requested a solution, in contrast to most people I work with who also seek conversation and understanding. I firmly believed that Frank did, indeed, need more experience with rejection, and that attempting to carry out the assignment would, at the very least, provide us both with useful information.

It also mattered that Frank is a sweet-looking, small-framed, white guy. I would not have given the same assignment to an African American or Middle Eastern man, because it would set him up for a racist response in the predominantly white Kansas City Country Club Plaza. Frank also has good common sense and is sensitive to the feelings of others. I was confident that he would follow the directive in a way that would not offend the women he approached. I relied on my clinical judgment and my intuition in trying out what was, for me, an unorthodox treatment approach.

While I'm not necessarily suggesting that you plant yourself at the bottom of the nearest escalator to conquer your own anxieties, Frank's story holds some important lessons:

*Action is powerful.* Sometimes you can move past a fear quickly, if you are willing to act. When you avoid what you fear, your anxieties are apt to worsen over time.

*Succeed by failing.* If you fear rejection, you may indeed need to accumulate more experience getting snubbed. This applies not just to asking someone for a date, but also to making sales calls, trying to get an article published, or approaching new people at a party.

*Risk feeling ridiculous.* Most people feel deeply ashamed at the very idea of appearing foolish, and shy away from taking healthy risks to avoid that possibility. Frank learned that feeling ridiculous— over and over—was tedious and uncomfortable, but not the primal threat to his dignity that he had imagined.

*Invite fear in.* When you anticipate a guest coming to visit, you are more prepared for whatever happens. Almost all treatments and strategies that help people with fear involve inviting fear in.

*Motivation matters.* If you're not at least a 6 or 7 on that 1-to-10 motivation scale, you may need to be in more pain about the status quo before you are willing to act. At the very least, you need to deeply feel the negative consequences of *not* acting.

An important postscript: If Frank hadn't had the motivation to carry out the assignment—or if he hadn't been willing or able to ask Liz out at this time—the experiment still would have been worthwhile. It would have given Frank and me useful information about his high level of anxiety and would signal the need for a different plan. Resistance to change can reflect the deepest wisdom of the unconscious. In many situations, our efforts to change have the best chance of succeeding if we proceed slowly and cautiously, with respect for how much anxiety we—or the other party—can manage.

But hey, a cure in a day? Some of us will take it.

## IT'S MORE COMPLICATED THAN THAT

In sharing Frank's story, I don't mean to imply that in the aftermath of a terrible loss, the bravest thing to do is jump into a new relationship. We all need time to grieve, and no single timetable fits all. Rejection is obviously hardest when we have intertwined the "dailyness" of our lives with the other person, when we have relied on that person for practical, emotional, and financial support, and when trust—including trust in our own good judgment—has been violated.

### "My Husband Walked Out on Me"

Mary's story is easy to identify with, even if the particulars don't fit your experience. Married for twenty years, Mary enjoyed what she considered a "problem-free" relationship with her husband until he left her for a coworker he had been sleeping with for more than a decade. She described her husband, Jeff, as "my entire life" and hadn't the slightest clue that he was involved with another woman until after he packed his bags and walked out. The aftermath of this rejection was profound, as Mary lost far more than her most significant relationship. She lost her identity and self-regard, as well as her sense of history, continuity, and meaning. Jeff's decision to leave, and his disclosure that he had had a lover for ten years, forced Mary to revise both her understanding of the past and her pictures of the future.

Because Mary had put all her eggs in the basket of one relationship, she hadn't strengthened her connections to family and
friends, nor did she have any plan to ensure her own economic survival. The end of her marriage was made even more painful because
she and Jeff had never talked about marital problems as they came
up; indeed, she had never even recognized the emotional distance
between them. So the loss hit Mary like an earthquake, utterly
without warning.

Understandably, sudden loss is more devastating and disorient-
ing than one we can see coming, try to make sense of, and plan for.
It is no wonder that Mary found herself overwhelmed by a crowd
of emotions, including rage, humiliation, shame, helplessness, and
depression. It was a sign of strength that Mary identified these
painful feelings, allowed them into her experience, and shared them
with me. She was also nearly frozen with fear.

When Mary told me of her greatest fears—that she would
never trust anyone again, or even want to get up in the morning—
I didn't give her a daunting directive, or even a small one. There
was no cure-in-a-day, even if Mary had wanted that, which she
didn't. What she wanted most was to share her pain and terror, and
to be heard. Very gradually, she began to confront what happened,
put Jeff's behavior in some kind of perspective, and look more objectively at her own denial of the distance that had long ago settled
between them. Tentatively at first, then with increasing confidence,
she began to act on her own behalf, which included making an
emotional and economic survival plan. Each of these moves required her to muster the courage to act in the face of anxiety. Finally, she took on the toughest, most fearful task of all—releasing
herself from her still powerful rage at her ex-husband. "I don't
know if I can do it," she confessed to me. "Why should I let him off
the hook when he was such a bastard?"

## The Courage to Let Go

When we are rejected, we may be frightened by our own rage. Later, like Mary, we may be frightened of letting it go. Years after a devastating rejection, we may resist moving forward because we are not yet ready to detach from our suffering. It's not that we take some twisted masochistic pleasure in feeling like the "done-in" partner. Rather, we may learn to wrap pain and suffering around ourselves like an old, familiar blanket. It can be our way of taking revenge—of showing other people how deeply they have harmed us through their outrageous behavior. To move forward in our lives may feel akin to forgiving the transgressor, to saying: "Well, I'm doing well now, so I guess your behavior didn't hurt me *that* much."

Then there's the fantasy that if we hang on to our justified rage and suffering long enough, the other person will finally see the light, realize how much he has harmed us, and feel as bad—perhaps even worse—as he has made us feel. It is a powerful and comforting fantasy. It is also just that—a fantasy.

Some of us may be afraid to let go of our anger because, in a strange way, it keeps us connected to the person who has hurt us. Anger is a form of intense attachment (albeit negative attachment), just like love. Both forms of emotional intensity keep us close to the other person, which is why so many couples are legally divorced, but not emotionally divorced. If you can't talk on the phone or be in the same room with your ex-spouse without feeling your stomach clutch, you're still attached. Detaching can provoke great anxiety—and require enormous courage.

When we let go of our anger and suffering (which does not necessarily include forgiveness) and begin to allow joy into our life, an odd thing may happen. We may temporarily experience anxiety and a sense of "homesickness" with every move forward. That's because with each step taken on our own behalf, we are taking emotional leave from a relationship that was officially terminated long ago. When we leave anger behind, we give up the dream that the person who harmed us will ever feel remorse, see things the way we do, or come back to us on his knees, pleading for another chance.

It took Mary a long time to let go of the secret hope that Jeff would return, abjectly apologetic. "Letting go" is not the same as avoiding real emotions. To the contrary, as Mary faced the loss of this dream, she experienced an onslaught of intense emotions, from heart-thudding anxiety to deep grief and loneliness, to, finally, a budding sense of energy and aliveness. Gradually Mary found that when she thought of Jeff, she no longer felt a knee-jerk surge of rage. Instead she was aware of a kind of quiet sadness—and on some days, a palpable sense of relief.

I don't mean to imply that we hold on to our anger because we consciously want to show the other person how totally she or he has screwed up our lives. Nor are these feelings completely in our control ("Gee, I think this would be a good time to let go of my anger and suffering"). I'm by no means saying that anger is "bad," since it can take great courage to acknowledge and express anger. But it requires just as much courage to free oneself from the corrosive effects of living too long with rage—a challenge that may include forgiveness but does not require it. What's clear is that nothing is served by ruminating about the terrible things your ex did to you, and making yourself miserable in the process, while he's having a fabulous day at the beach.

## NO ONE ENJOYS REJECTION

Both Mary and Frank suffered the profound loss of being abandoned by the person they believed to be their life partner. Not all hurts cut so deep. But regardless of the particulars of a relationship, I have yet to meet a person who enjoys being rejected.

I still remember when I was sixteen and my best friend dropped me for another girl, which I took to mean that I wasn't "deep" enough for her. This friend was my soul mate, and when she rejected me for another best friend (whom I imagined to be far more interesting and complex than I), the injury and loss were immense. I felt devastated, my confidence crushed. It is a great relief to be grown up, to have a number of close friends instead of one best friend, and most importantly, to not take rejection so personally. Or, at least, to be working hard at not taking it so personally.

When we take rejection as proof of our inadequacies, it's hard to allow ourselves to risk being truly seen again. How can we open ourselves to another person if we fear that he or she will discover what we're trying desperately to hide—that we are stupid, boring, incompetent, needy, or in some way deeply inadequate? Obviously we won't meet many people's standards or win their affection, respect, or approval. So what? The problem arises when shame kicks in and we aren't able to view our flaws, limitations, and vulnerabilities in a patient, self-loving way. The fear of rejection becomes understandably intense when it taps into our own belief that we are lesser than others—or lesser than the image we feel compelled to project.

Rejection is a fast route back to childhood shame. It's not just that you went to a party and no one made an effort to talk to you. It's that you're essentially boring and undesirable, and so it is and so it will always be. If you engage in this sort of global thinking you may avoid intimacy entirely by never truly allowing yourself to be seen, or known. Or you may defensively reject people or situations because you fear that once you're seen for who you really are, you will be deemed unworthy and unlovable.

You may even believe that the person who does the rejecting is automatically superior to the person who is rejected. Relationships are not some sort of bizarre competition in which the person who gets out first, refuses to attach, or suffers less is proclaimed the winner. Rejection can reveal just as much, and often more, about the insecurities and fears of the person doing the rejecting.

We might all wish to don armor (or at least a wet suit) to protect us from the feelings of shame, self-loathing, depression, anxiety, and rage that rejection can evoke. None of us is immune to the pain of rejection, but the more we grow in maturity and self-worth, the less likely we are to take it quite as personally. When we acknowledge that rejection is not an indictment of our being, but an experience we must all face again and again if we put ourselves out there, rejection becomes easier to bear. The only sure way to avoid rejection is to sit mute in a corner and take no risks. If we choose to live courageously, we will experience rejection—and survive to show up for more.

# CHAPTER 3

# Terrified?

*You Have to Keep Showing Up!*

Therapist David Reynolds says: "When people tell you they don't fly because they're afraid of flying, you need not believe them. They don't fly because they don't buy airline tickets."

On many occasions I have felt anxious or frightened and I've decided that I won't let fear stop me from showing up and doing what I need to do. Flying is a good example. Like many women, I became terrified to fly, or more accurately, terrified to crash, after having children. Waves of anxiety would wash over me at night as I pictured my little boys' faces and then imagined my plane, engulfed in flames, plummeting to the ground, leaving them grieving and motherless. These fearful imaginings began days before every departure.

People often calm down by going for the facts. My friend Miriam, for example, has had no heightened anxiety about flying since 9/11. But she has always feared that her plane will be struck by lightning. Her anxiety was considerably lessened when I gave her an article on this very subject, which said that the last con-firmed commercial plane crash in the United States directly at-tributable to lightning occurred in 1967. The article also stated that even if a bolt of lightning happened to strike a plane, "nothing should happen because of the careful protection engineered into the aircraft."

Back in my own fear-of-flying days, this article would not have encouraged me. "Nothing *should* happen," I would have said to my husband, Steve, and anyone else who would listen. "What the hell does it mean that 'nothing *should* happen' if lightning hits the plane? Why didn't this expert say, 'Nothing *will* happen'?" I would have been inconsolable.

Even after I felt comfortable flying alone or as a family, I insisted that Steve and I protect our boys from orphan status by flying sep-arately for about twenty more years. This terribly inconvenient practice made no logical sense. I would insist on separate planes for Steve and me, then drive with him from the airport to our hotel in a cab with broken seat belts and a thick sheet of glass separating us from the driver that would have inflicted a major head injury in the event of even a minor accident. Some of the cabdrivers appeared to be on drugs and/or to harbor homicidal tendencies. Had I been even a teensy bit rational, I would have flown with Steve and in-sisted that we take separate ground transportation.

Back then, my friends' cheerful reminders that air travel is the safest way to go did not at all reassure me. No amount of statistical evidence could compete with the terrifying scenarios I concocted in my head. Nor was it my spiritual belief that if my plane went down, it was part of some divine plan. Neither science nor faith put me at ease.

I was cured because I kept buying airline tickets—in short, I kept showing up. I haven't always been as spunky in other situations that scare me, but my work demanded a fair amount of travel, and the consequences of not flying would have been intolerable for me, both personally and professionally. Things become less terrifying the more we face them, and each time I got off a plane intact, I felt a little more capable of managing my fear. I flew so much that my fear eventually melted away. Experience gave me comfort where reasoning had failed.

## FEARS VS. PHOBIAS

If my fear had reached phobic proportions, I would have availed myself of the best treatment program or medication I could find. A genuine phobia, which happily I did not have, comes complete with a racing heart, breathing difficulties, sweating, an overwhelming need to flee the situation, and sometimes an imminent fear of death. It causes enormous suffering. A phobic individual is gripped by paralyzing neurochemical storms that render advice like "feel the fear and do it anyway" totally irrelevant. Nor does it help to tell a phobic person to take a Valium and wash it down with several inflight cocktails while repeating to herself that air travel is safer than driving.

People often use the word "phobic" to describe ordinary fear and trembling. "I'm phobic about flying," a client told me just this morning. He's a white-knuckle flyer who feels an adrenaline rush when the pilot announces that he's putting the seat-belt sign on because he anticipates some choppy air. My client hates takeoff and landing, and he gets a mildly upset stomach whenever he flies. He also tortures himself with a certain amount of preflight catastrophic thinking. But he doesn't have a true phobic reaction to flying. If he did, he wouldn't be able to board a plane in the first place.

If you or someone you know has a genuine phobia, the good news is that it can be treated and overcome. This is especially true if you have a specific phobia, though help is also available for panic attacks that strike for no apparent reason, and for social phobias involving a paralyzing fear of social or work interactions. Treatment is important because avoidance won't work—in fact, it makes things considerably worse. Research demonstrates that the harder phobics work to avoid the things they fear, the more their brains grow convinced that the threat is real.

If you're not phobic but merely terrified, avoidance also makes the problem worse. Like Frank in the preceding chapter, you need some experience with the very activity you dread, be it dating, driving, or raising your hand in a meeting. But only you can judge what you're ready to take on. If you jump right in, you may learn that the fearful imaginings cooked up by your overactive brain never come to pass. Then again, they might. I refuse to reassure people that the universe really is a safe place and that you should always trust it. If you push past your fears, bad things may happen.

Consider my adventures at the podium, where I confronted my fear of public speaking. It's a bit like buying a plane ticket. You say yes to an invitation because it's way off in the future. Then the future shows up and you're supposed to show up, too. Public speaking rarely results in a fatality, but, as my podium adventures will illustrate, it does offer wonderful opportunities for public humiliation and shame. Which, we will see, can be its own reward.

## SPEECHLESS IN SEATTLE

Several years ago, I stood before an audience of Seattle psychotherapists, about to begin a lecture on the topic of women and intimacy. After several impromptu comments, I glanced down at the podium to begin my formal presentation. At that moment my most dreaded fantasy materialized. My prepared talk had disappeared.

Waves of anxiety washed over me. There I stood in front of hundreds of people who had left the comfort of their homes and had paid a considerable sum to hear me talk—and now I had no talk to give. Minutes earlier, I had placed the only copy of my talk on the podium, and then retreated backstage while being introduced. But when the person who introduced me finished, she carried away both her introduction and my talk. She then rushed out of the building to another engagement.

At other times in my public speaking career, I have been entirely sure of what I wanted to say—but got it all wrong. Once, in Portland, I opened a lecture by saying, "I'm so happy to be here with you in Denver this evening." It was the next-to-last stop in a seventeen-city book tour, and I was beyond exhausted. Several women in the front row yelled back at me, "Portland, Portland!" They were trying to be helpful, but I stood there on stage and stared at them blankly. Why, I wondered, were these women yelling "Portland" at me?

Then there was the lecture in Berkeley where I tossed my head in an infelicitous fashion, snagging an earring on my wool suit jacket. My right ear was pinned to my shoulder, and despite my best efforts, I couldn't extricate myself. After several minutes of silence and fumbling, I was rescued by a relative who ran up on stage to release me from a position that I have otherwise assumed only while doing neck rolls in yoga class.

During my early years of public speaking, I also suffered more than a few plain, old-fashioned anxiety attacks. Since I couldn't predict when nausea, tachycardia, or other symptoms of terror would strike, I worried nonstop about it happening. Shortly before going on, I would huddle backstage with my manager, Jo-Lynne Worley, and whisper urgently: "I can't do this. Why am I doing this? Nothing is worth going through this. I will never do this again." Jo-Lynne, who had heard this litany before, would respond calmly, "You'll do great. You've done it a million times," whereupon she'd remind me to breathe and push me on stage in the direction of the podium. My evaluations invariably included comments like, "Harriet is such a warm and relaxed speaker." But even the most enthusiastic audience response did little to reassure me the next time around.

## Your Worst Fantasy May Happen!

Public speaking ranks right up there with snake handling and death on the list of activities that grown men and women most dread. But unlike snake handling and death, public speaking is something that many people want to do—but don't dare to. I know, because folks tell me so. When I ask people what stops them, I hear one or another "neurotic fantasy"—their words, not mine—about the hazards of facing an audience. ("You'll think I'm crazy, but I have the recurring dream that I'll be up there and suddenly I won't have my lecture notes.") Of course, these folks are not crazy. I can offer no glib reassurances about the perils of public speaking. In fact, it's clear to me that if you do enough lecturing, your worst "neurotic fantasy" is highly likely to become reality. I was quite lucky in Seattle: I had given versions of that particular speech several times before, so I could wing it without too much trouble. At other times—many other times—my blunders have been unmistakable and irretrievable. Mishaps, I've come to realize, are simply part of the lecture-circuit territory.

## The Gift of Gaffes

The inevitability of my podium faux pas didn't mean that I had to consign myself to a career of dodging public speaking opportunities. The secret to managing onstage anxiety, I've discovered, is to stop viewing your goof-ups as intolerable humiliations and begin to see them as useful, perhaps even essential, elements of an effective public presentation. Improbable as it may seem, bumbling can be powerful.

I made this discovery several years ago in Chicago, where I was to give a keynote address based on my new book at the time. I had every reason to feel confident about my upcoming performance. I had carefully prepared my talk. I had insisted upon, and received, a state-of-the-art laser pointer that I felt would help me get my ideas across more effectively. Not incidentally, I had borrowed an elegant suit jacket from a friend that was more professional-looking than anything I could find in my own closet. What, I thought, could possibly go wrong?

I found out almost instantly. As I strode out before the audience and placed a copy of my speech on the podium, I failed to notice that this particular lectern lacked the conventional ledge for holding papers. The pages of my speech cascaded to the floor. This incident might have been relegated to the category of minor embarrassment had it not been for the fact that I had not bothered to number the pages. Unlike my Seattle speech, this was a brand-new presentation, and I wasn't yet familiar with its flow and structure. "Just a minute," I said brightly, then spent the next five shuffling papers and trying to control my panic. At last I was ready to begin.

Ten minutes into the speech, I broke the expensive laser pointer that I had borrowed from my hosts. Keeping my sense of humor about it became difficult when, a few moments later, the left shoulder pad of my silk jacket somehow lost its moorings and came to rest up against my neck. "Breathe," I sternly ordered myself, but by now I was beyond the reach of oxygen therapy. I finished my talk in a stew of embarrassment and wondered if I should drastically lower my fee for future (if any) speaking engagements. But my trials were not over. During the question-and-answer period, I was forced to respond, "I don't know" several times. "Some expert," I berated myself.

Then, mercifully, it was over, and I busied myself for a moment at the podium, gathering up my speech in preparation for a quick getaway. When I lifted my head, I saw to my surprise that a small crowd of women had gathered around the lectern. They were smiling at me. "*Thank* you," said one, reaching out her hand to shake mine. "It was wonderful to see you being so real." A younger woman, a psychology graduate student, chimed in. "I've always been afraid to speak in public," she confessed. "Now I feel, if you can do it, I can do it!" Others spoke of the palpable connection they felt with me during my talk, a sense of being in the presence of someone whom they already knew and understood. Being approached by members of an audience following a speech wasn't a new experience for me. What was new, however, was the level of vitality and connectedness I felt flowing toward me that evening. I looked around at the open, loving faces surrounding me and felt my embarrassment melting away.

## THE PERFECTION TRAP

One reason that public speaking is so terrifying is that it's hard to feel we have the right to be ourselves—flubs and all—at the lectern. After all, the podium has historically served as a place for an elite group of men to reflect themselves at twice their natural size. It has never been a place to admit ignorance, confusion, or even complexity. To stand at a podium is to elevate oneself—literally—above other humans. To pretend to have all the answers and to never drop one's papers, break a pointer, or, God forbid, lose track of a shoulder pad.

But what I found out on my Night of a Thousand Screw-Ups, and countless times since, is that audiences don't just tolerate mistakes; they actually can be inspired and invigorated by them. After my blunder-fraught speech, the women in the audience no longer had the option of idealizing me. Instead, it was as though they could now see a reflection of themselves in me—both the schlepp and the successful woman that reside within me. If I was simultaneously a vulnerable, mistake-prone, and competent woman, then perhaps their own limitations weren't as important and defining as they may have believed. The women I talked with seemed exhilarated by this knowledge and, ultimately, so was I.

## Honor Your Stage Fright

Don't get me wrong. I still haven't entirely transcended my fear of public speaking, and there is an excellent chance that I never will. To this day, I prefer to stand when someone is introducing me, so that I won't get dizzy and pass out in the process of rising from my chair. And each time I approach the podium, I still want things to go perfectly. The truth is that I have an uncommonly high schlepp factor—a seemingly limitless capacity for spillage, breakage, tripage, and collisions with inanimate objects. No one chooses to be a schlepp in front of a large audience. When I goof, I still entertain fantasies that the stage floor will open up and swallow me whole.

But I also honor the fear and trembling that continue to seize me before each public presentation. Stage fright is often characterized as a form of narcissism, a crippling overfocus on the image of the self that one presents to the world. But I believe that the opposite is true. I have come to view speech anxiety as a sign of fundamental integrity. It seems to me that those of us who face our audiences with weak knees and fluttering innards understand too well the essential humanity that we share with our audiences. We know in our bones that we are no better or more evolved than the people who sit before us, yet we are being invited to pretend just that. The podium's mandate: Fake infallibility and aim for perfection. To approach an audience in the face of that demand—even when we disbelieve it—is a harrowing experience.

Public speaking sure did teach me a thing or two. I learned that I'm never going to transcend fear, but I needn't let it stop me. I learned that survival is a perfectly reasonable goal to set for myself the first dozen or so times I face a dreaded situation. I learned to observe my worst mistakes in a curious, self-loving way. I learned to hang on to the life raft that is my sense of humor. I learned that I must show up. Finally, I learned to view my worst failures as a gift to my sisters and brothers, who, upon observing my glaring imperfections, might gather the courage to get behind the podium themselves.

## WHAT PUBLIC SPEAKING HAS TAUGHT ME ABOUT PRIVATE SPEAKING

Actually, the risks I've taken behind the podium are minor compared with the vulnerability I feel when I open up a difficult conversation with someone in my personal life. Public speaking, after all, is a hit-and-run affair. Even if you've made a total fool of yourself, you know you'll never have to face those people again. They'd rather listen to you anyway than be home cleaning the kitchen or figuring their taxes. Plus, the people who come to hear you will be far more forgiving of your foibles than they would if you were a brain surgeon or even, say, a concert violinist. And if your prepodium anxiety becomes more than you can bear, you can simply choose to turn down public speaking invitations. But none of us can avoid *private* speaking—the anxious conversations that take place with the most important people in our lives. We cannot *not* communicate with those individuals, because even our distance or our silence conveys something.

I'm happy to say that hanging out in front of large audiences has given me some tools for communicating better with people in my personal world. Allow me to digress by sharing a few lessons I've gleaned from my public-speaking career that may apply to your personal conversations when the emotional climate is anxious or otherwise intense.

- Establish a connection with your listeners by schmoozing about the easy stuff before leaping into a difficult idea that makes you (and others) nervous. If you can make people laugh early on, so much the better.

- Make clear that the subject at hand matters to you, but keep in mind that talking about a serious subject doesn't require you to convey your message in heavy, morose tones.

- Let others draw their own conclusions. If you address people with missionary zeal—suggesting that if they don't agree with you they're deeply misguided and may go straight to hell—you'll lose them.

- You'll also lose them if you go on for too long.

- Figure out when you can be spontaneous and wing it, and when to do your homework, prepare, and even rehearse.

- Meet people wherever they are. Yes, you can make the exact same point to your cousin who is the administrative director of the Berkeley Gay and Lesbian Student Coalition and your uncle who heads the Christian Coalition for Family Values. But you can't make that point in exactly the same way. It's not that you're aiming to be a wishy-washy, accommodating chameleon. But if you want to be heard, you must help others feel at ease.

- Treat every question and comment with respect. It never helps to shame people or make them feel stupid—even when they're trying their darnedest to do that to you.

- Don't pretend to have all the answers. It's fine to say, "That's an interesting idea. I'll think about that one." People actually like it when you indicate that you're human.

- You can't *make* anybody hear you. Your daughter may be paying rapt attention to your every word, or she may be fully absorbed in contemplating the ceiling or entertaining her private sexual fantasies. Your primary focus should be on what you want to say and how to best say it, rather than on needing a particular response from the other party.

Whether I'm facing an audience of fifteen hundred or an anxiety-provoking conversation with a friend, I find it helpful to remember an incident from my childhood. I grew up in Brooklyn, New York, not far from Coney Island. Whenever I visited the amusement park, I was both terrified and enticed by a ride called the Cyclone, a daunting, high-speed roller coaster. Over several summers, I watched kids about my age get on and off that ride. I stood by as an observer, amazed by their fearlessness.

One day a particularly sweet-looking boy strapped himself into the first car. When the ride was over, I approached him. "How did you do it?" I asked bluntly. "How did you get over being afraid?"

"You don't get over it," he told me. "You just buy a ticket."

And remember to breathe.

## CHAPTER 4

# In Praise of Anxiety:

*How Fear and Trembling Keep You Safe*

I'm on the phone with my friend Emily. She is a deep thinker.

"Say something profound about anxiety," I demand.

"It doesn't feel good," Emily says flatly. I knew I could count on her to cut to the heart of the matter.

"Think positively," I insist. "How has anxiety helped you? Give me a specific example."

"When I get anxious about money, my anxiety helps me cut through my avoidance," Emily observed. "So I take care of business. Getting anxious at the right time keeps me out of trouble."

While no one enjoys feeling anxious, the experience of anxiety can be protective and life preserving. Just as physical pain tells us to get our hands out of the fire, our fear tells us—once we've been burned—to be cautious about fire the next time around. The fight-or-flight response that anxiety evokes can save our lives—that is, if either fighting or fleeing happens to be the wisest thing to do in the face of a present danger.

Anxiety is a warning sign that can stop you from doing something stupid. I remember hearing a sad story about a young man who was killed while whitewater rafting. Word had it that he used an inferior-quality raft and ran an intense rapid that was beyond his level of expertise. A friend of mine, a skilled outdoorswoman, summed up the tragedy in one sentence: "He died because he didn't have enough respect for the water."

I heard "respect" as another name for fear. Perhaps this man hadn't been sufficiently afraid. Or maybe he felt the fear and did it anyway. Of course, we know nothing about this guy, except that if he *did* feel fear, he didn't let it stop him. And he died.

Fear—if we attend to it—can also protect us as we navigate the rapids of personal relationships. It can signal that we are about to do too much, too soon. The body registers every level of anxiety, including the most subtle, subliminal cues that warn us not to act. You may feel a prickle of dread as you contemplate confronting your sister, because the time is not right to do so. Perhaps, to proceed wisely and well, you need to slow down or make a new plan. You may feel like a coward when your anxiety pushes you to choose silence over speech, or restraint over action. Yet in many circumstances, silence and restraint are the wiser, more courageous choices.

You also need to pay attention when your anxiety tells you *to* act. Perhaps you should trust your gut that something is indeed wrong with your baby, even though two different doctors have told you that nothing is wrong, and that you're just an anxious, overprotective mom. Maybe you are a mother who *does* worry excessively— but you still may be right. The fact that you're anxious about your child's health may push you to persevere in a medical system that is shaming you for doing so. Even if your anxiety turns out to be misguided, it's to your credit that you've gathered enough opinions and information to reassure yourself that you've done all you can.

Because anxiety is a signal to pay attention, denying our gut reactions in certain situations is unwise. My own inclination as a mother was to overreact in nonproductive, anxious ways. But the time that I got the most holes punched in my Bad Mother card was the night I denied my anxiety and refused to acknowledge the big red flag waving in my face.

## I SHOULD HAVE THOUGHT "ZEBRAS"

It was May 1978, and I was in Atlanta for a speaking engagement. On the Saturday night following my talk, Steve called the hotel baby-sitting service to get someone to stay with Matthew, then our only son, who was not yet three. When the baby-sitter showed up at the door of our hotel room, my reaction was not positive.

Actually, I would not have wanted to spend five minutes with this individual. She was an emaciated, visibly agitated, unkempt woman in need of a bath. She wore layers of drag queen–style makeup, and although she avoided eye contact, I noticed her eyes had a glassy, distant look. But Steve didn't look nervous to me, nor I to him, and it would have been very awkward to send her away, plus we were using a service in a fairly upscale hotel, and surely they had some standards.

It was understandably difficult to put our heads together in the hotel room to strategically change plans, but we should have done so the moment we stepped out of the room and closed the door behind us. Instead we hailed a cab to the restaurant and went inside before we looked at each other and said, almost simultaneously, "Let's get out of here."

In the cab on the way back to the hotel, my denial metamorphosed into near panic. I remember thinking that I would never,

ever forgive myself if Matthew was harmed or missing, because I had registered "something wrong" in no uncertain terms but had pushed the anxiety aside. My own profound discomfort at judging someone by his or her looks or appearing prejudiced against the mentally ill and addicted (the person may have been both) sealed the deal. To avoid the terrible embarrassment of righting the situation by sending the sitter away, I pushed my anxiety underground and off we went. I should add in our feeble defense that this was the seventies when neither of us had ever heard of a nanny or baby-sitter harming a child.

We returned to find Matthew and the sitter tensely poised on the edge of the bed, watching television. Every parent knows the dizzying rush of relief that comes when the child you thought was in danger is actually safe. At least the incident taught me humility. To this day, when a mother is demonized by the media for doing some horridly neglectful thing, I don't feel on higher ground. I feel only lucky. Had things gone differently, I can just hear myself on the witness stand, telling the judge, "Well, yes, I really did think that something was terribly wrong with this baby-sitter. Yes, I felt creeped out by this person. Yes, this person could well have been high on drugs. Yes, I am trained as a clinical psychologist. But, you know, the situation was just so . . . well, *awkward,* that I convinced myself it was okay to leave."

Doctors are taught that when you hear galloping hoofbeats, "first think horses, not zebras." When it comes to parenthood, Steve thinks horses. I think zebras. When Matthew and Ben lived at home, I was a frequent visitor to the land of catastrophic thinking. If, say, my boys did not arrive home at midnight when they were due, my rational self knew it was unlikely that they had been kidnapped or that they were lying in a ditch by the side of the road after being hit by a drunk driver. But these possibilities would occur to me, sometimes with the accompanying adrenaline jolt and sick feeling in my stomach.

In contrast, such dire possibilities did not seem to occur to Steve. When Matthew drank and peed endlessly during a ball game one night in Kansas City, I thought "juvenile diabetes." Steve thought "thirsty." Generally speaking, I'd prefer to be like Steve, since it's often better to underreact than overreact to life's uncertainties. But on that night in Atlanta, at least one of us needed to register that a zebra had entered the room.

Needless to say, our anxiety—or that powerful bodily sensation that we sometimes call a "gut reaction"—doesn't always help us to act wisely. We can misread the signals, sensing danger where none exists. We can respond from a place of prejudice, defensiveness, cowardliness, misunderstanding, old hurts, or fear of differences. Or we may simply be a high-strung, emotionally sensitive person, meaning the fear center in our brain is too easily jolted. But when our gut registers something is not right, it's a good idea to pay attention.

Let's look at two more examples of how anxiety can serve as an important warning signal in a relationship. Both touch on the issue of sexuality—a high-twitch issue for almost everybody in this culture.

## CAN I TRUST MY HUSBAND?

Joan, a woman I saw in psychotherapy, felt very anxious about her husband's close "platonic friendship" with Ingrid, a female coworker in his computer business. When Ron casually told her that Ingrid would be joining him at a weeklong workshop on "Dreams and Spirituality" in another city, Joan felt even more threatened, especially as the subject matter was obviously unrelated to computers.

"I'm so upset that she's going to be there," Joan told me with obvious distress. "But what can I say?" After all, her husband had signed up for the workshop six months earlier and had asked Joan if she wanted to attend, an invitation she had declined. Certainly Ingrid had the right to attend whatever conference she pleased. Joan initially concluded that she was overreacting.

But no matter how hard Joan tried to "think positively," her anxiety continued to escalate. She pictured her husband having a deep spiritual experience with his "friend," leading to more workshops together, more intimacy, and, ultimately, to an emotional or physical affair that would shatter her marriage. In tears, she shared this frightening image of their future with her husband. Appearing stunned and affronted, Ron wrote off her reaction as irrational. "Maybe Prozac would help," he suggested.

Joan's spiraling anxiety may have been fueled by many factors, including betrayals of trust that she had experienced in past relationships, going back to her first family. To her credit, she didn't want to sabotage her marriage with neurotic fears or obsessive ruminations about worst-case scenarios, which was why she had brought up the issue in therapy. Together, we looked at some important questions. Had she experienced irrational abandonment fears in previous relationships? Did she have a history of unexpected loss, for example, the untimely death or disappearance of a parent or sibling? Had any key person left her "out of the blue"? Did close friends and family members think she had abandonment issues that predated her relationship with Ron? Had she distrusted previous partners who were trustworthy? Did she see herself as an especially jealous or mistrustful person? Joan needed to consider other factors that might be fueling the intensity of her anxious response.

## Trust Your Gut—and Get the Facts

Investigating our anxiety can be an intricate and subtle process. On the one hand, revisiting the pain of the past can help us move forward into the future without confusing a current relationship with people and events from our history. On the other hand, a history of loss doesn't necessarily mean that our current relationship fears are groundless. Joan, for example, came to recognize that her father's sudden death when she was thirteen had made her especially sensitive to abandonment. Certainly she needed to be aware of that special vulnerability, so that she wouldn't overreact to her husband's, or anyone else's, behavior.

But Joan's sensitivity to loss didn't mean that the Ron-Ingrid problem existed only in her imagination. No marriage is affair-proof, and anxiety (like anger, jealousy, and other forms of emotional intensity) can signal that something is not right.

While Ron insisted that there was no sexual or romantic attraction between him and Ingrid, he may have been lying to Joan (otherwise honest people lie about sex and take their sexual secrets to the grave). Or he may have been lying to himself. Even if nothing had been going on between Ron and Ingrid, it would be wildly naïve to imagine that their relationship wouldn't change if the two of them were thrown together in close quarters. And to go off to a weeklong conference on "Dreams and Spirituality" (compared to, say, a brief workshop to learn a new computer system) would put Ron and his close friend in an environment in which intimacy could easily flourish. When Joan took a hard look at these realities, she recognized that her anxiety about the upcoming workshop most likely did reflect her good instincts rather than some off-the-charts possessiveness.

Paranoia and knee-jerk jealousy can rear their heads in any relationship. But so can anxiety that signals that something is truly amiss. In Joan's situation, underreacting would surely be as problematic as overreacting. Most people in couples, even those who place a high value on individual freedom, want their feelings to be considered, and expect some healthy reserve in their partner's other intimacies. The fact that Joan's anxiety persisted, combined with her assessment of the real risks of the situation, ultimately prodded her to honor her feelings.

At first, Joan did nothing but stomp around in angry protest, which made Ron more stubbornly defensive about his plans. Finally, she was able to approach her husband with an open heart and share just how threatened she felt, and how intolerably scary the situation felt to her. She asked him to cancel his plans to go to this particular workshop, while recognizing that the final call was his. For the first time, Ron heard the pain and vulnerability behind his wife's pleas. He ultimately chose not to go.

The crisis also led Joan to look squarely at the low level of closeness, engagement, and zest in her relationship with Ron. She had been moving through her marriage like a sleepwalker. Now awake, she began to pay serious attention to warming things up, and she moved toward her husband in a more loving, playful, and respectful way. While Joan suspected she had *over*reacted a bit to her husband's friendship at work, she had *under*reacted to the entrenched distance that had settled into her marriage.

Nor had she ever asked Ron direct questions about his attractions to other women that would help her to know her husband better as a sexual person. Sexual attractions that are denied by one partner ("I only want *you*, honey!") are more likely to be acted upon than attractions that are discussed frankly with a partner. Real trust is built on mutual self-disclosure and knowledge about one's partner, which for some couples includes knowledge about the other as a sexual person. When Joan finally gathered the courage to ask Ron about his attraction to other women, at first he denied it vociferously. But when she shared that she had been drawn to two other men over the last several years—though she hadn't acted on her feelings—Ron admitted that he, too, had felt a "little pull" toward other women from time to time. Toward Ingrid? Joan calmly asked. Ron was silent for a moment, and then slowly nodded. "Maybe a little bit."

## Our Emotional Barometer

On a daily or even moment-to-moment basis, anxiety plays a crucial role in helping us to negotiate the opposing forces of separateness (the "I") and togetherness (the "we"). Our anxiety signals us to seek more connection when too much distance sets in, and to seek more space when the togetherness force is too intense. There is no "right" amount of closeness or distance for every couple, or even for the same couple over time. We automatically make moves toward more togetherness and more separateness, even within a single day or hour.

Excessive anxiety pushes us to extremes—that is, we glom on to the other person like Velcro, or we defensively wall ourselves off. Or two people get polarized, so that one is locked into the role of the pursuer, the other the distancer. A smaller dose of anxiety, however, can be a useful barometer in our efforts to get comfortable, serving as a sign that we are in danger of too much remoteness—or, alternatively, suffocation.

## DO I TRUST MY THERAPIST—OR MYSELF?

It's perhaps hardest to accurately "read" our anxiety and discomfort in a relationship where the power balance is unequal, making one person more vulnerable than the other. Marriage is often such a relationship. Psychotherapy is always such a relationship. If we seek help from a therapist or counselor, what do we make of the anxiety and discomfort we may feel? Is anxiety simply a normal part of the process? Is it a signal that we need to protect ourselves? Or are we just being neurotic?

Sonia felt mired in these questions when she came to me for a consultation. After meeting six times with a psychiatrist for depression, she told me this:

> Dr. S. looks at me and talks to me in a way that makes me uncomfortable. I feel there's something seductive or sticky about him. In our last meeting he said that I was a very desirable woman and that I wasn't able to accept my sexuality. I was just talking about wanting to lose weight, and I felt his comment was out of the blue. When I got up the nerve to share my discomfort, he said that I was pushing him away because I had been sexually abused as a child. The abuse is why I'm there—so maybe I can't trust myself. My gut says leave, but Dr. S. warns me that I'll get worse if I shop around for a new therapist. My husband is also encouraging me to stay because he's heard good things about this doctor.

Sonia had many questions. "Is it possible that I'm distorting reality? Am I 'resisting' therapy? Can I hurt myself by leaving?" It made sense that she was struggling. Starting therapy is an anxious business, so an individual's fears, fantasies, and projections can easily run amok. It's not easy to be objective about therapy or a particular therapist. So, yes, Sonia could be distorting—as could anyone in her shoes.

Nonetheless, I encouraged her to trust her gut reaction. The fact that Sonia had a history of sexual abuse was absolutely no reason to discount her current feelings and perceptions. Indeed, her painful history may have sharpened her radar, helping her to be especially sensitive, alert, and self-protective. I responded that since she felt unsafe and uncomfortable in the sessions, she should seek a consultation with one or more therapists until she found someone with whom she did feel safe and comfortable. The fact that this particular psychiatrist had a stellar reputation said nothing about whether he was the right person for Sonia. Nor is reputation or status a guarantee of competence in this line of work.

I'd advise anybody to be wary of a psychotherapist who warns that you will get worse if you try another therapist or treatment. A good clinician will share an honest perspective while respecting your wish to "shop around" so that you can gather the facts that will allow you to make the best treatment decision on your own behalf. Even if Sonia were fleeing therapy in response to irrational fears, she would not hurt herself by leaving. If she later discovered that she had made a mistake by leaving this psychiatrist, she could always call him and ask to resume the work. If he didn't welcome her back, or if he shamed or intimidated her for wanting to leave in the first place—well, she shouldn't stick around with such a doctor. Sonia *can* hurt herself by staying when her gut reaction tells her to get out.

Sonia's decision to honor her anxiety proved to be an act of strength and courage. She found her adult voice to tell her psychiatrist that although it was possible she was distorting, she didn't think the therapy was a "good fit" and she planned to leave and consult with someone else. When Sonia was abused as a child, she didn't have the power or the ability to say, "No, this is not right for me. I am leaving. I am going to protect myself." Children can't take control of an unsafe situation. But as an adult Sonia could—and she did.

## FEAR AS FRIEND

Throughout evolutionary history, anxiety and fear have helped every species to be wary and to survive. Fear can signal us to act, or, alternatively, to resist the impulse to act. It can help us to make wise, self-protective choices in and out of relationships where we might otherwise sail mindlessly along, ignoring signs of trouble.

A good dose of anxiety about our mental or physical well-being may motivate us to seek help or make a difficult change. A health scare, for example, may get us to eat differently, exercise more, and reorder our priorities. A reminder of our mortality can awaken us from a psychic slumber and inspire us to be more clear-eyed and awake, readier to figure out what really matters. If we don't pay attention to a gentle warning, we may get a more insistent message that we need to make a significant change on behalf of our own well-being. Perhaps we may need to do less—or more—for a family member, pursue a passion, or leave a job that is slowly killing us.

Anxiety can force a more honest self-appraisal, including a good look at whether we are living in accord with our core values and beliefs. But while fear can inspire us to make an important change, it may not help us to sustain the change over time. It just gives us a good start. When fear eventually subsides, we need to draw upon our own clarity, strength, resolve and grit to stay on course.

Perhaps you can think of additional ways that anxiety is a useful emotion. For example, anxiety can tap you on the shoulder, or deliver a bone-shaking jolt, if you happen to contemplate robbing the nearby convenience store—or consider any other behavior that fundamentally violates your values and beliefs. The capacity to feel anxiety plays an important developmental role in the establishment of what we call "conscience" and the capacity to experience healthy guilt. In this regard, anxiety can work as a kind of social glue, spurring us to treat others fairly and kindly even when our impulses are less than benevolent. Likewise, healthy anxiety in others can prod them to treat *us* well.

On an entirely different note, anxiety can spice up our experience when it's part of a larger picture of novelty, eroticism, romance, adventure, performance, or any new challenge. In the right dose, it can heighten the moment and give a certain "edge" to our performance. We gain a sense of mastery when we undertake something that entails a risk and "survive."

Even when anxiety takes entirely miserable forms (which it often does), it can teach us something. When we share our anxieties and fears with friends and family members, we can learn how to receive comfort and accept help from others. By opening ourselves up and accepting support, we also help them to feel less alone or ashamed about their vulnerabilities and imperfections. In the process, we enhance our own capacity for empathy and compassion, because, well, we've been there. We know that anxiety can make anybody lose sleep, memory, and concentration; feel dizzy or nauseated; shake uncontrollably; or totally freak out. It's simply part of the human experience.

Sharing the more vulnerable parts of ourselves is one way we feel intimate with others. I know several people who have never visibly shown anxiety or spoken openly about their fears in the long years I've known them. I have come to love and admire several of these people, but I don't feel especially close to them. While I might seek out such a person to be my pilot or dentist, my best friends are people who share their anxious moments and worst fears as generously as their talents and competence. It's the open sharing by both parties that, for me, keeps the relationship balanced and intimate.

## ANXIETY DEFICIENCY DISORDER?

Not surprisingly, the diagnostic manual of the American Psychiatric Association has many labels for people who struggle with anxiety.

These "mental disorders" include generalized anxiety disorders, panic disorder, post-traumatic stress disorder, social phobia, object-specific phobias (blood, elevators), hypochondria, obsessional worrying marked by anxiety and distress, and compulsive behaviors (like counting, checking, cleaning) aimed at magically preventing some dreaded event. That's the short list. The suffering it encompasses is real enough.

Yet, interestingly, we don't have similar diagnostic labels for folks who fail to get anxious when they should. True, one can get diagnosed with a "conduct disorder" if one's behavior is sufficiently deceitful, aggressive, and destructive that it violates the social codes of family and society. But what about the less flamboyant ways that many folks operate at the expense of others, or themselves—and don't get the internal signals to change course? What about people in positions of power who harm others in their single-minded pursuit of profits, never feeling much anxiety about their behavior? Or ordinary citizens who go about their business as usual and fail to register or respond to dangerous, unfair, or downward spiraling events in their families, communities, or global environment? I'm not suggesting that we all live awash in anxiety at the state of the world or our own relationships. In fact, when we get too anxious we lose our ability to be good problem solvers. But it's interesting to think about the fact that when anxiety disrupts functioning, it is considered a psychiatric illness. There is no diagnosis for indifference, the most dangerous emotion of all.

CHAPTER 5

# The Trouble with Anxiety:

*How It Wreaks Havoc on Your Brain and Self-Esteem*

How nice it would be to always see fear as a solicitous friend—a natural survival mechanism that warns us to keep the door shut when the wolf is waiting outside, or primes us to fight, flee, or freeze when the wolf has found his way in. In the face of imminent danger, we need to react—not stop and ponder the pros and cons. So hurrah for all the ways anxiety can keep us safe, attuned, intuitive, and alert as we watch out for ourselves and those we love.

As we've seen, fear *can* be a positive force *if* it occurs at the right time and in the correct dose, *if* it helps us connect more deeply to our shared humanity, *if* we "read" it correctly in order to cope with a current challenge or future threat, *if* it serves as a positive motivating force or simply adds zest to our lives. But these are big "ifs."

For the most part, our instinctual responses to anxiety no longer fit the stresses of modern times. More often than not, we're not facing a wolflike threat. Most stresses we face today require us to slow down, limber up our brain, and do our best problem solving. When we're too anxious we won't be able to gather new information, think clearly about the problem, explore our options, give calm and clear feedback to others, and find creative solutions that consider the needs of all. And fear can run amok, flooding our system with adrenaline and hijacking our neo-cortex—the thinking part of the brain.

## ANXIETY IS A MEAN TRICKSTER

Usually, anxiety is a mean trickster. It signals you to pay attention, but it also turns your brain to oatmeal, narrows and rigidifies your focus, and obscures the real issues from view. Anxiety tricks you out of the "now" as you obsessively replay and regret the past and worry about the future. It tricks you into losing sight of your competence and your capacity for love, creativity, and joy. It tricks you into believing that you are lesser and smaller than you really are. Anxiety interferes with self-regard and self-respect, the foundation on which all else rests.

It makes no difference whether you view your anxiety as a product of your genes, faulty brain circuitry, early trauma, current stress, world events, or the moon and stars and grace. Whatever your perspective, one thing is certain: Anxiety can make you feel dreadful about yourself. It can impede your capacity to think. It can dig a big negative groove in your brain and make it impossible for you to hang on to a positive thought for more than five seconds. It can affect your body in ways that can feel crippling

### Get Me Out of Here!

When anxiety has you in its clutches, you will want to move out of your body and inhabit some other space—anything to escape that awful feeling. Regrettably, there is no place to go. You can't vacate the premises.

When anxiety gets really bad, prepare to shake; hyperventilate; feel nauseated; throw up; get dizzy, sweaty, antsy, jittery, tense, irritable, agitated, or otherwise hyper-aroused. You may have difficulty swallowing and feel a constant lump in your throat. In bed at night, you may grind your teeth and jerk your legs like an overcaffeinated marionette. You may breathe too rapidly, hold your breath, or feel as if you might stop breathing entirely if you don't force yourself to inhale and exhale. You may call 911 convinced that you are having a heart attack—or that you are losing control and going crazy. You may feel numb, faint, physically immobilized, exhausted, detached from your body, and, at the same time, unbearably stuck in it.

What harms you is not the dreadful way that anxiety feels in the body, whether it's moderate agitation or a full-blown panic attack. We are all capable of managing the most anguishing physical sensations when we know what is happening to us, when we understand that what is happening is frightening but not really dangerous, when we know we won't die from it, and when we know that eventually the feelings will subside. But when we develop a fear of fear itself, we're lost. Certain that we "can't stand" to feel this way, we try hiding out from fear, running from it full speed, or fighting it off with a big stick. Doing any of these things only makes fear grow bigger and stronger—and makes us feel smaller and weaker.

The more you try to make fear go away (an impossible dream), rather than learning to function with it, the worse you will feel about yourself. You will let fear stop you from doing what you need to do. You will mistakenly see yourself as a weak and impaired individual, rather than as a strong, competent person who happens to have an overactive fear response.

## Anxiety and Your Brain

When you're *really* anxious, your thinking center may shrink to the size of a pinto bean. It's obviously hard to feel good about yourself when anxiety disrupts your memory and concentration, leaving you unable to read, write, study, analyze, or take in new information.

I am quite familiar with the experience of anxiety turning the brain to mush. I'll bring Steve or a friend along to any important medical appointment because I know that my mind is apt to race, go blank, flood, or freeze. Also, my sense of direction, shaky in the best of circumstances, is especially vulnerable to the brain-numbing effects of anxiety.

Once, when my younger son, Ben, was attending middle school, I was called at work to come immediately and take him to the hospital. Steve was out of town. The school nurse told me that Ben was reporting the following symptoms: His right hand was numb and the numbness was spreading up his arm, his vision was impaired ("words were coming off the page"), he was having difficulty speaking, and he had vomited. A brain tumor, I thought. My son has a brain tumor. Then I flashed on Ben's earlier stint in the intensive care unit of the local hospital, as a result of a skateboard accident that had caused a frontal lobe concussion. It's *worse* than a tumor, I concluded. Maybe a blood clot related to the concussion had dislodged itself and Ben would die shortly. Or maybe he was having a stroke. Did the school nurse think Ben was having a stroke? Should I call 911? The nurse suggested I simply come to school and pick up my son.

I headed toward the school sick to my stomach, searching for any medical explanation less disastrous than the ones I had come up with. But nothing else seemed plausible. I got lost on the short drive to the school and was a puddle of emotions by the time I arrived. The hospital, which I knew well, was only a couple of minutes away, but I doubted my ability to find my way there, locate the emergency entrance, park, and sign my name. So I grabbed Sheila, the school social worker, and all but dragged her out to my car to guide me to the hospital, despite some person in authority shouting after me that this was not Sheila's job and that she really needed to stay on the school premises.

Ben did not have a brain tumor, a migrating blood clot, or stroke. On that terrifying day, he had his first migraine-from-hell. This possibility didn't occur to me, since I knew almost nothing about migraine headaches, which, I have since learned, can mimic serious neurological symptoms. Ben's migraines *were* from hell, but this diagnosis was a huge relief, as you might imagine.

In a crisis, most of us can readily identify anxiety as the culprit behind our poor mental functioning. In these situations, we can usually forgive ourselves for our temporary brain-lock and move on. But when anxiety operates as a chronic, underground force, we may fail to identify it as the culprit behind our poor functioning. We just feel bad about ourselves, which, of course, revs up our anxiety even more.

Anxiety scrambles the brain in other ways that leave us feeling helpless and self-doubting. As we've all experienced, anxiety promotes catastrophic thinking. When you're anxious, doom-and-gloom fantasies tend to permeate your day, and reach a fever pitch when you're lying in bed. Your anxious mind, saddled with far too much free time in the wee hours of the morning, will hook on to some dire, worst-case scenario—frequently on the subject of personal finances, health, your child's future, or the state of the world. My point is not that catastrophic imaginings are necessarily irrational. Anything *can* happen. But these thoughts grip you in a way that accomplishes nothing except to make you feel miserable and powerless.

Anxiety also can destroy your capacity to tolerate ambiguity and complexity. You can't see two sides of an issue, much less six or seven sides. Most devastating to your self-esteem is that the ability to see the many-sidedness of your *own self* is lost. You tend to get locked into a narrow view of who you are, and lose sight of your own possibilities.

## Losing Perspective

Consider Eliza, who came to see me for therapy feeling like an emotional basket case. Eight months ago her mother had died of a heart attack, and her dog, her best pal of thirteen years, had died only weeks later. Since that time, Eliza had lost all sense of her competence. She expressed feelings of utter helplessness and the conviction that she would never be able to handle what came her way. She told me things like "Something is wrong with my mind" and "I just can't learn new things." She also shared that she felt ugly, pathetic, unlovable, and weak. At the age of thirty-six she was convinced that her chances for happiness were over, and that she would never accomplish anything worthwhile.

Eliza was now avoiding social situations and new opportunities to learn. Avoidance, of course, only made her feel worse about herself and increased her fear. While Eliza had always been shy and self-conscious, her sensitivity to criticism and disapproval had now spiraled to intolerable proportions. She told me, for example, that while she was walking toward a restaurant with several women from her workplace, she tripped on the pavement. It was a trivial fall. She picked herself up, brushed herself off, and told her coworkers she was fine. But she felt so horrible ("There was no *reason* to fall. I tripped over *nothing*") that she had hardly been able to eat her lunch. She knew, objectively speaking, that her coworkers had not thought less of her for tripping. Still, her conviction that she appeared ridiculous stayed with her throughout the day—and beyond. Eliza began eating alone in her office.

Eliza had read a book on the anxiety disorders, and even before our first meeting, she had diagnosed herself as having a "social phobia." She also knew that losing her mother was an emotional event of vast proportions, complicated further by the major blow of her dog's death. She had made a connection between these profoundly stressful events and the loss of self-esteem she was experiencing. In these ways Eliza was ahead of the game. She recognized that the awful things she said *to* herself *about* herself were merely symptoms of anxiety, shame, and depression rather than essential truths.

## EVERYONE HAS AN ANXIETY DISORDER

If you are alive, you have an anxiety disorder. This is not to say that you are feeling as debilitated as Eliza or that you meet the criteria for a psychiatric diagnosis, as Eliza did. And by expanding the category of "anxiety disorder" to include us all, I do not mean to trivialize or erase the profound suffering of those who suffer from severe, relentless anxiety, paralyzing panic attacks, post-traumatic stress disorder, and phobias.

But anxiety affects the way each of us perceives ourselves. As author Susan Jeffers reminds us, anxiety activates the little chatterbox in our heads that spews out catastrophic scenarios and serious doubts about our ability to cope, do new things, and handle whatever life brings. It drives our "lower-self" thinking, which spurs us to operate from our most reactive self. So, if you want to sign up for a ceramics class or give a dinner party or move to another city, your anxious mind will immediately counter with several reasons why you're inadequate to the task and shouldn't try it or, for that matter, even think about it for another moment.

A vicious cycle ensues. In the face of anxiety (even the anxiety we're not aware of), we tell ourselves we can't cope with whatever the new challenge is. We let fear stop us. Fear then grows bigger and stronger, because nothing is more frightening over time than the feelings of helplessness and powerlessness that come from inaction, avoidance, and a commitment to sameness.

We are all in the anxious soup together. As long as we are alive, anxiety will interfere with the accuracy of our experience of self and others. We may not even recognize anxiety for the trickster it is, because anxiety erodes the essential human capacity to *think about our thinking*. In realms both personal and political, we don't observe that anxiety has locked us into a narrow, rigid, simplistic, "good guys vs. bad guys," quick-fix mentality. In fact, we may confuse our anxiety-driven reactivity with doing our best thinking. Anxiety will have this reality-distorting effect whether it washes over us like a tidal wave or operates as a silent thrum below the surface of our daily lives.

## COMPARISONS, COMPARISONS, COMPARISONS!

Anxiety revs up *judgmentalness* and *criticism*. When directed toward the self, these often take the form of negative comparisons. To some extent we all compare ourselves to others. It's easy to come up short because we compare our insides with other people's outsides, and while we know our own worst selves, we never fully know the pain, vulnerability, and sadness of others.

Comparisons are inevitable, because most self-assessments—am I generous, gifted, clumsy, accident-prone, funny, boring?—are made through an implicit comparison to some socially constructed norm. Sometimes comparisons spur us on to better ourselves. But when comparisons drag us down—or when they're unrelenting—that's an anxiety-driven response.

## My Sex Drive, My Self

Consider Jane, a therapy client of mine. Today she tells me about the "sex talks" she's been having with two of her girlfriends, who describe their uncontrollable lusts and wildly ecstatic orgasms in great detail. Jane knows there is a range of "normal," and she's aware that her friends may exaggerate. Plus, they are single and she's been married for eight years. But still, Jane tells me she feels ripped off and preoccupied by her low sex drive. These days, she can't get past it.

I'm struck by Jane's narrow and singularly negative focus on her biologically ordained sex drive, as she sees it. First of all, many emotional and relational forces influence her capacity for sharing and sustaining an intimate physical connection with her husband. Nor can "real sex" be defined by the strength of orgasm alone. Some women can achieve a strong orgasm in a mechanical or impersonal manner, but may be unable to enjoy kissing, cuddling, petting, gazing into their partner's eyes, or having a loving and playful connection in bed. Other women may be able to enjoy fully giving themselves over to the moment and to their partner through touching and pleasurable skin contact that doesn't lead to orgasm.

As for biology, Jane may well fit the research on low-testosterone ("low T") women that relationship expert Pat Love describes so well. Dr. Love (her real name), a self-proclaimed low-T person herself, gives a funny and accurate description of what it takes for a low-T person to "get going" after the altered brain chemistry of the honeymoon stage wears off.

First, you have to focus, focus, and focus some more, until you get exactly the right erotic fantasy in mind. Then, of course, a spot on the ceiling or a thought about the laundry distracts you, and you have to start working all over again until finally, *finally*, you get to the point of orgasm. Your actual orgasm, if you want to get competitive here, may be every bit as impressive as that of your high-testosterone partner, but it's a lot different getting there. You're probably not going to be the one to initiate sex—or if you do, it's out of love and altruism, not out of desire. For the low-T person, desire takes some effort to come by (pun intended) once the initial sexual "high" of an intimate relationship wears off.

Jane's observation that people differ widely in the ease and intensity of their sexual experience is accurate, whether particular friends exaggerate or not. People also differ widely in their capacity to enjoy nature, art, friendship, work, sports, conversation, humor, theater, and horses. I've worked with Jane long enough to know that if she weren't feeling ripped off by her sex drive, she would find something else to wrap her brain around in a negative way. It's what she does when she's anxious and stressed. Her automatic thoughts might be "If only I was as brilliant and gorgeous as Marie, then I'd be happy and fulfilled." Or "I haven't made any contribution to the world compared to my friend Arlene," or "No one would really love me if they truly knew me." Anxiety—even when we're not aware of feeling anxious—generates this kind of downward-spiral thinking.

It's not the fact of who Jane *is* that causes her pain. It's her thoughts. As her therapist, I'm curious about "why now?" That is, what has narrowed Jane's attention to her "inadequate" sex drive at this point in time, when the culture has long been saturated with images of women slipping effortlessly into ecstatic, orgasmic sex?

The "why now?" question is relevant to all of us. You probably know from personal experience that your sense of yourself can be remarkably fluid. You might feel unable to articulate a complete sentence at a staff meeting, then be irresistibly witty that very evening as you compose an e-mail to a good friend. You can feel pulled down by your reflection in the mirror one morning, and think you look pretty good the next day. You don't really shrink from a size 16 to a size 12 in one day, so what else is going on?

In Jane's case, it turned out that she had a lot on her plate. We all have times in our life when stresses converge—when we're dealing with one crisis and the universe sends us another while we're down. Jane was struggling with whether to leave a job she hated, and fearful about how she would survive and what direction her life would take if she quit. Her husband was about to be laid off, and Jane's current work setting, a social service agency, was coping with dwindling resources, struggling with survival anxiety, and acting like one big dysfunctional family. I also reminded Jane that she was coming up on an important anniversary date, as her daughter turned six  the age that Jane was when her father had a serious heart attack. The degree to which Jane gets down on herself in a judgmental way is a good measure of the amount of stress she's under, and a signal that she needs to redirect her attention toward identifying and working on the real problems.

As for dispiriting comparisons, the reality is this: There will always be folks who have more of something (better sex, a larger apartment, easier children) than we do. Likewise, there will always be folks who have less. Both the "have-more" and the "have-less" groups include people who live vital, joyful lives, as well as folks who feel chronically bitter, cheated, and unhappy. Having more of something we want can make life a lot easier, but it won't bring us meaning, happiness, or self-regard. Jane needs to step aside from comparisons, or, more realistically, to learn to strip them of their emotional power.

## Why Are You Putting Yourself Way UP There?

While anxiety drives feelings of worthlessness and incompetence in some people, it inspires narcissism and grandiosity in others. So a high dose of anxiety may inspire you to be a big know-it-all. You may be convinced that if it weren't for your ceaseless bad luck, not to mention the incompetent people you work with, you would already have been awarded the Nobel Prize. At slightly milder levels of anxiety, you may simply think you possess the truth of the universe, and anyone who thinks, feels, or behaves differently is misguided or wrong. It's your job to fix them.

If you recognize yourself here, you may be entirely unaware that underground anxiety fuels your defensive sense of superiority. You may mistake your anxious reactivity for doing what is necessary or helpful, for giving people what they need or deserve. That is, you *overfunction*.

## Doing Too Much, Doing Too Little

Feeling essentially superior to other people is as sure a sign of poor self-esteem as feeling essentially inferior. They are merely flip sides of the same anxiety-driven loss of balance. If you overfunction in relationships, you are likely to feel self-righteous or "one-up." If you underfunction, you are likely to feel self-doubting or "one-down." Let's define our terms.

If you *overfunction* under stress, you may

- Feel you know what's best, not just for yourself but for others as well.

- Move in quickly to advise, rescue, mediate, and take over.

- Have difficulty sitting back and allowing others to struggle with their own problems.

- Avoid anxiety about your own personal goals and problems by focusing on others.

- Have difficulty sharing your own vulnerable, underfunctioning side, especially with those who are viewed as having problems.

- Be labeled the person who is "always reliable" or "always together."

If you *underfunction* under stress, you may

- Have several areas where you just can't get organized.

- Become less competent under stress, thus inviting others to take over.

- Tend to report physical or emotional symptoms when stress is high in your family or job.

- Become the focus of gossip, worry, or concern.

- Earn such labels as "the fragile one," "the sick one," or "the lazy, incompetent one."

- Have difficulty showing your strong, competent side to intimate others.

Overfunctioning and underfunctioning are automatic ways that we respond to stress and try to dampen our own anxiety, especially when we don't have a clue about where the real threat lies or what to do about it. As with pursuing and distancing, our particular style of managing anxiety in relationships is not good or bad, better or worse. Each style of managing anxiety has both positive and problematic aspects.

When overfunctioners and underfunctioners pair up (which they usually do), the pattern or "dance" between them is problematic, because each person's style of managing anxiety provokes and maintains the other's. If you overfunction for an underfunctioner, that person will underfunction even more. Ditto for pursuers and distancers. If you pursue a distancer, he will distance more—and vice versa. It's an unfortunate irony: The ways we navigate relationships to relieve our personal anxiety in the short run only make things more stressful in the long run.

When anxiety hits, pursuers and underfunctioners are more likely to feel and report low self-esteem than are distancers and overfunctioners. Those who pursue and underfunction carry more of the anxiety and are more likely to be seen as "the problem" in the relationship. But the difference is more apparent than real. The challenge in each case is to observe one's own style of managing anxiety, then to move the self and your relationships toward more wholeness and balance.

Of course, we may both overfunction and underfunction, depending on the context and circumstance. When anxiety hits, I underfunction in the realm of practical, "real-world" skills (say, following written instructions or getting Ben to the hospital). I may have difficulty accessing more than a thin slice of my competence in terms of noticing and doing what needs to be done. On the emotional/relational scene, my tendency under stress is to overfunction, which may take the form (if I don't curb it) of judgmentalness, a preoccupation with what someone else is doing wrong, and unsolicited advice giving.

## Why Doesn't She Shape Up?

Here's a personal example of my tendency to judge and overfunction with friends.

I treasure my friends, I count on them, I love them unabashedly, and I call them terms of endearment like "sweetums" and "honeybunny." When I am feeling calm and centered, I simply appreciate who they are, and truly feel that their limitations and vulnerabilities only add to my experience of their uniqueness and what I can learn from them. At such times, I resonate with the words of Anaïs Nin, "Each friend represents a world in us."

But at other times I can get riveted on some limitation of a particular friend, or how she is screwing up (so I believe) a relationship. At such moments, I may have to restrain myself from offering unsolicited advice to whip her into shape. If I'm feeling strongly enough about her "problem," I may begin talking to that friend in my head and telling her what to do. Better that I do it in my head, because I can be obnoxious when I offer unsolicited "truths" to my best friends when my own underground anxiety inspires me to enlighten them.

For example, a friend in Berkeley complains constantly to me about her partner, whom she fails to stand up to. She feels "done in" by his controlling behavior, but whenever I encourage her to speak up, she will say things like "It only makes things worse" or "You don't know Bill!"

When I am calm, I can discern her participation in the marital pattern with great clarity, but I don't need her to be different. I can be creative in expressing my perspective in a way that will maximize the chances she will hear me, but I also understand that my friend may have more at stake in maintaining the status quo with her husband—or more at risk in challenging it—than I can appreciate.

If I find myself obsessing on a particular day about my friend's spineless behavior, I know that this response is a red flag warning me that I am anxious and stressed out about something else I'm not attending to. Overfocusing on what others are doing wrong, and getting reactive about it, is a common, automatic anxiety response.

So I try, instead, to figure out what other issues might be fueling my judgmental response on a particular day. Is it related to feeling stirred up about my father, who would never speak up or take a position on anything that mattered? Am I feeling bad about myself or worried about the future? Is there something else I'm feeling anxious and stressed about that I'm not paying attention to?

When I'm anxious, I get instructive. So I've learned to wait (at least most of the time), to see whether the need to speak endures over the course of a day or two. Usually the intensity dissipates because it's being driven by my own stress. Waiting also allows for a clearer intuitive response on my part about how to put things and whether even to bother. My motto in the face of anxiety: *Strike when the iron is cold.*

Obviously, not all forms of intensity are anxiety-driven. If you pay attention, you can distinguish between an anxious, uncentered sort of intensity and the passion—the fire in the soul—that lends energy and zest to love and work. But the amount of time you spend ruminating about someone else's bad or misguided behavior is an excellent measure of your own level of stress, whether or not you are aware of what's stirring you up.

## What's Your Anxiety-Driven Mantra?

Being judgmental of others often takes the form of obsessive thinking. For example, we may have our own personal, anxiety-driven mantras that go round and round like an automatic tape. These repetitive thoughts often center on the experience of being mistreated or done in. Your mantra might be: "My sister cheated me out of Dad's money," or "I can't stand my brother's drinking," or "My ex is turning the kids against me."

Whether you are right or not is beside the point. Such anxiety-generated thinking is totally nonproductive, flushing your valuable time and energy down the tubes. Ditto for anxiety-generated thinking that takes the form of judging yourself and your future in a negative, doom-and-gloom way. If you pay attention to your body and observe your thoughts, you can begin to distinguish thinking that comes from a calm center and leads to problem solving from an anxious, ruminative overfocus on a person or problem that goes nowhere.

## THE FOUNDATION OF SELF-ESTEEM

Good self-esteem rests, first and foremost, on having an objective, balanced perspective on our strengths and weaknesses. We all have plenty of both. But anxiety and fear push us to extremes, so we may feel like an emotional basket case on the one hand, or present ourselves as having no needs, problems, or loose ends on the other. Anxiety, by its very nature, will lead you to lose objectivity about the complex, wonderful, flawed, ever-changing person you are. When you can't see yourself objectively, you won't see anyone else objectively, either.

Good self-esteem also requires that we view our vulnerabilities and limitations with curiosity, patience, and humor. Nobody is perfect, and we can all benefit from working on ourselves. But the process of self-observation, reflection, and change is basically a self-loving task. It will not flourish in an atmosphere of terminal seriousness, self-flagellation, or self-blame.

Unless you are a saint or a highly evolved Buddhist, you will partake in a fair amount of anxiety-driven judgmentalness of both yourself and others. Keep in mind that the tendency to be judgmental—toward yourself or another person—is a good barometer of how anxious or stressed out you are. Judging others is simply the flip side of judging yourself.

### Living the Life We Have

Authentic self-regard doesn't come from comparisons or one-upping anybody. Nor is it the inevitable outcome of a loving, secure, and stable childhood, should such a thing exist. Solid self-esteem in adulthood is hard earned. It comes from tapping into our own creativity and personal pleasures, from developing our competence and our connections, from participating in friendship, intimacy, and community. It develops from living in accord with our deeply held values and priorities, from learning to recognize and share both competence and vulnerability, and from navigating relationships with integrity, balance, and generosity of spirit. Living well is the work of a lifetime that demands our full attention.

Every human life is unique, and every human life has value. We're not meant to be anyone else but ourselves. We all face the challenge of living the life we have, not the life we imagined having, the life we wish for, or the life we are quite certain we deserve. So we need to do whatever it takes to let go of anxiety-driven judgments and comparisons. Life is short, and none of us really has that kind of time.

In truth, you will always be vulnerable to feeling essentially inferior or superior to others. When anxiety hits, it's what humans do. But you can observe it and get perspective. Anxiety will never go away, but anxiety is not you. You are much larger, stronger, and more complex than anxiety, mean trickster that it can be. When you lose your sense of competence, optimism, and well-being, when you get critical toward yourself or others, when you feel essentially "better than" or "inferior to" others, when you feel the discomfiting physical effects of anxiety or the miserable symptoms of panic—stop and remind yourself that it's just anxiety doing its thing. It can help enormously to simply recognize the many faces of anxiety so that you don't confuse it with your whole self.

## Snapping the Rubber Band

A number of practices and techniques are available to help you loosen the grip of judgmentalness, or any type of anxiety-driven,

unproductive thought pattern. I'm not a technique-oriented therapist, but I'm always interested in learning from my therapy clients
what helps.

One woman, Katy, tells me about a technique for managing her
unwanted judgmental thoughts about herself and others. She
learned it from a women's magazine she came upon at her hairdresser's. The article suggested a "rubber band technique" for stopping thoughts. Katy has elaborated on the technique, using her
imagination and self-knowledge to create a tool that works for her.

Here's what she does: When Katy finds herself drifting into
negative thinking, she snaps a rubber band on her wrist and says to
herself in a spirit of playfulness, "Hello again, you silly little critical
thought! How are *you* today?" If she's alone, she may say this out
loud. Then Katy puts the thought in an imaginary red Dumpster
and lets it ride down a railroad track where it gets dumped into a
pile at the end of the track. She doesn't try to stop the thoughts
(which is impossible), but she's found a way to say howdy to them,
and to use her wonderful sense of humor to give each judgmental
thought—these days focused on her "loser brother"—a little welcome and sendoff.

Katy doesn't think too much about *why* her brain wraps around
"negative thinking" at one point in time and not another. Her belief
is that the variations in her thought patterns have more to do with the
vicissitudes of her "weird brain chemistry," as she calls it, than anything psychological. No matter. Katy has a gift for silliness, and this
technique, combined with daily aerobic exercise, has so far offered
her the best relief in loosening the grip of unwanted thoughts.

Calming her brain frees Katy to be more creative in approaching
the relationship problems she does want to explore. When relationships get stuck in too much distance or blame, you can be sure that
anxiety is the driving force. The capacity to calm down and think—
rather than automatically react—is where real change begins.

Katy, for example, is working on observing and modifying her tendency to overfunction with her younger, underfunctioning brother. When anxiety and stress hit, her automatic response is to give advice, offer help, and even bail him out. Then she moves into a position of distance and blame when he doesn't appreciate or make use of her efforts or even bother to show up. That's when she gets stuck in compulsive ruminations about all she does for him and how manipulative, dishonest, and irresponsible he is.

Katy is learning that *not* being helpful—and reducing her expectations to zero that her brother will change—is the best way to be helpful. She's also working on staying warmly connected to him, as she sets limits rather than distancing. ("I'm sorry I can't loan you money. I'm feeling concerned about what I might need in the future.") She is learning not to lecture, moralize, or criticize, as she clarifies what she can't do for him. Even when he asks for advice, she is learning not to have the answers for him. ("This is what I might do, but it may not fit for you.") This is a difficult and long-term project—far more challenging than snapping a rubber band.

If Katy can stay with it, she will lower her anxiety and feel on more solid ground as a person. And "staying with it," when we are making changes that don't win us love and approval, is the ultimate test of our courage. This is because the process of change requires us to tolerate a great deal of short-term anxiety for the long-term rewards.

# CHAPTER 6

# Why We Fear Change

Two things will never change: the will to change and the fear of change. Both are essential to our well-being and to the preservation of our relationships. We all move back and forth between our desire to learn, risk, experiment, and grow—and our anxiety about doing so. Change brings loss in its wake, even when it's a change we truly and deeply want to make.

I have a story I love to tell. When my younger son, Ben, was six years old, and my first book, *The Dance of Anger*, was published, I overheard him exclaim to a small friend, "Do you know that my mother worked on her book for my *whole life?*" It was true enough. And while I had accomplished a great deal during the years it took to complete the book and get it published, what had Ben accomplished during that same period? From a bawling infant without language, comprehension, or any coherent sense of self, he had transformed himself into a distinct six-year-old personality who used the toilet and was knowledgeable about some of the innermost workings of the New York publishing scene. Now that's change!

"Wouldn't it be wonderful," I sometimes muse to friends, "if adults could hold on to that extraordinary capacity for change and growth?" I recently visited friends whose two small children are fluent in French and Spanish, just from exposure to these languages. I couldn't help but be envious.

But in truth, it would be terrifying if we, as adults, changed as much as children during those early years. We'd all be awash with anxiety and engulfed by a grief so large it couldn't be contained because there would be no stability and cohesiveness in our lives at all. We would have no moorings, nothing to keep us tethered to this earth.

We count on a high degree of sameness not only in ourselves, but also in the people we care about. No matter how much we may complain about our difficult brother or critical mother, we still count on the fact that they will be pretty much the same person the next time we visit them. We may want them to change—but only so much, and only in the ways we desire. Others feel similarly about us. It's not just the capacity to change, but also the capacity to *resist* change, that stabilizes our sense of identity, our continuity with the past, and our connections with others.

## CHANGE: WHERE WILL IT ALL END?

Change is an anxiety-arousing business because whenever you make a change, you can't make *only* one. There is no guarantee where it will stop. You may decide, for example, to assert yourself by telling your husband that you intend to become more knowledgeable and involved in the family finances. Or you may insist that instead of spending next summer at his parents' cabin in Wisconsin for the third summer in a row, you want him to accompany you to a remote island off the coast of Greece for an archaeological dig. If you truly hold your ground (that is, if you feel fully entitled and you really mean it), you may discover that seven or thirty-two other marital issues will begin to rear their heads.

Your husband may say, "No, we're going back to the cabin, because my parents insist on it and they'd be devastated if we don't come every year." Perhaps you begin to see more clearly that you are married to a man who is unable or unwilling to take a stand with his own parents—and that the cabin is only one of many issues. What do you do next? Do you take a firm position and say, for example, "I admire how much you care about your parents and I don't want to hurt their feelings. But I'm not willing to spend every summer at the cabin, so let's figure out what we're going to do." And if your husband replies, "We're going to the cabin, end of conversation," then what? Do you tell yourself he's such a difficult man there is nothing you can do but accommodate? Do you suggest that he go to the cabin and you'll go on the archaeological dig with your best friend? Do you tell him that you need to have an equal vote in the decision-making department, whether it's about where you vacation or other major issues? Do you retreat into resentful silence, or do you think creatively about how to keep the conversation going over time?

The more you find your own clear, strong voice in the relationship—and figure out what's negotiable and what's not—the more you will test out how much capacity your husband and your marriage have for change. Of course, he may surprise you and say, "Wow! An archaeological dig in Greece! That's great!" Then *this* new adventure may bring new learning that also threatens the predictable status quo in your marriage, creating more anxiety.

## Cooking School in Tuscany

I worked with a couple in therapy who had been married for several years. Almost from the beginning of their relationship, Craig and Janet had settled into rigid, complementary roles. He was the leader, the teacher, the competent one, while she was the follower, the pupil, the childlike one. By idealizing her husband as a brilliant man, someone whose intelligence was out of her range, Janet had been able to bury her anger at her constant accommodation and at Craig's pedantic, know-it-all style.

At Craig's suggestion, they enrolled in a cooking school as part of a vacation in Tuscany. There they discovered that *she* was the more comfortable and competent traveler in every respect. Janet's Italian improved by leaps and bounds, while Craig's did not, nor did he even try to speak the language—save the occasional *buon giorno!*—to avoid appearing foolish. Janet turned out to be the star pupil in cooking classes and, apart from that, caught on to everything quickly, from understanding the exchange rate for money, to connecting with local folks, to planning offbeat day trips. Craig struggled to take any initiative at all. Rather than expressing his insecurity or anxiety openly, he became irritable and judgmental about Italy and about travel in general. "We already live in a city that offers more sights and cultural events than we can ever sample in a lifetime," he complained to Janet. "I can't see the point of traveling four thousand miles to spend this kind of money."

By the time they got home, the old equilibrium of the marriage had been shattered. Janet found herself becoming more forceful about a host of issues—such as how and when to eat, socialize, spend, save, and travel—rather than automatically deferring to Craig. Even in small matters, she became more assertive. For example, when they would see a movie together and Craig would deliver an analysis as if it were the last word in film critique, Janet would gently tease him— "Might there be room for another opinion here?"—then state her own. She started seeing both herself and Craig more accurately, rather than holding on to the belief that her husband's "brilliance" rendered the intellectual gulf between them fathomless.

If this couple hadn't traveled to Tuscany that summer, perhaps other life events would have destabilized their polarized roles. To their credit, they courageously weathered a lot of marital conflict and found creative ways to renegotiate a host of marital issues. Ultimately, Craig was grateful that Janet dragged him into new territory, even when he initially went kicking and screaming. It was her spunk and expansiveness that had attracted him to begin with, and some part of him wanted to let go of his burdensome, perpetually in-charge role. But the process could easily have spiraled downward were it not for their maturity and strong commitment to each other.

Every new place we visit—be it a foreign country, a budding friendship, a child's birth, or a new job—evokes a new world within us. To avoid the anxiety inherent in change and growth, we may doggedly cling to the familiar. By clutching tightly to the safety of sameness, we may try to keep everyone and everything as sure as sunrise and as fixed as the stars. But it's not possible. Life is process, movement, and transformation. Try as we may to "hold back the dawn," change is the only thing we can count on for sure.

## NECESSARY LOSSES

Thumbing through the diary I kept during my senior year at Midwood High School in Brooklyn, I found these words: "Finding is losing something else. I weep, even mourn, for that which I lost to find this."

I have no memory of where I found this quote or what inspired me to inscribe it for posterity, but I'm sure it's not a coincidence that I recorded it when I was preparing to leave my home in Brooklyn to attend college in Madison, Wisconsin. Second to being born into this world, I was about to embark on the most dramatic change of scene I had ever encountered. I pictured myself about to become an "entirely new person." Choices would sprout, possibilities bloom, and the question that goes hand-in-hand with change—Who knows what might happen?—both intrigued and scared me.

Rereading my diary entries (always a humbling experience), I noticed that the fears I listed were pretty mundane. Would I be popular? Would I be smart? Would I get a good boyfriend? Would I get along with my roommates? Would I get the classes I wanted? But the quote I penned in my diary spoke to a larger anxiety. Learning is finding. Finding is losing something else.

It's obvious that we all fear failure and the challenge of coming up against our own limitations. Less obvious are fears about going "too far." What if new ideas challenge our habitual, comfortable ways of working and turn us into "beginners" again? How do we hold on to the people we love if we become too different from them? What if new learning challenges cherished beliefs that have anchored us and kept us close to people who are important to us?

## Unconscious Loyalties

The more "set" we are in our thinking and in our relationships, the more we may fear that diving into new learning will destabilize old beliefs and important relationships. We may then hold ourselves back without even intending to do so.

Claire, an extremely talented therapist I know, had a wonderful and distinguished mentor during her psychiatric residency. This man advised her, taught her, protected her, and fostered her growth. He and his wife also included Claire in family occasions. When the time came, he scouted job possibilities for her and wrote glowing letters of recommendation. Ultimately, he found her a staff position in the prestigious hospital where he ran the outpatient unit.

Obviously, Claire was lucky to find a mentor—a fairy godfather of sorts—to help her find her way in her professional world. But his influence turned out to be a mixed blessing. She had become so attached to her mentor, and so indebted to him, that she closed herself off from new ideas and directions that conflicted with his beliefs and thereby might threaten their special relationship. When she was offered a chance to train in a new form of mind-body psychotherapy that deeply intrigued her, she turned down the opportunity, convincing herself she was simply "too busy." Such unconscious loyalties are powerful. Some of the smartest men and women I know have abandoned their best, independent thinking to protect their bond with a mentor, a teacher, a therapist, a spouse, a parent, a boss, or a group of colleagues.

Change is an anxiety-arousing business, both for the one doing the changing *and* for those affected by the change. Often we fear that another person's move toward new ideas and experiences will create a gulf so wide that we will not be able to reach them. This anxiety can arise in any relationship, but as the following story illustrates, the particularly intense bond between mothers and daughters can make a venture into new territory especially harrowing—for both parties.

## "SO WHAT'S WRONG WITH THE PERSON YOU WERE?"

During our first therapy session, Marion told me that she thought she might have the "fear of success" syndrome that she'd read about in a women's magazine. On the afternoon she made a major breakthrough in writing her doctoral dissertation, she feared she was having a heart attack. She had been stuck for weeks, writing and rewriting the introductory section without success. One morning, however, she awoke with a new idea and began writing with clarity and ease. She became so excited about her breakthrough that she began to think about turning the dissertation into a book and making a valuable contribution to her field. Later that afternoon she began to have dizziness and chest pains and drove herself to the ER.

"I know this sounds crazy," Marion said to me, "but I was convinced it was all over. I said to myself, 'Well, that's what you get. That's your punishment for trying to get a Ph.D. That's what you get for thinking you're so smart—for being so full of yourself.'"

Marion came from an Irish working-class family, where having a "swelled head" and drawing attention to oneself—positive or negative—were taboo. Marion was the first woman in her entire extended family to attend college, and her mother, Fiona, who had badly wanted her daughter to be educated, had gradually begun to respond to Marion with put-downs and wisecracks. When Marion got a scholarship for graduate school, she excitedly told her mother that education was turning her into "a whole new person." Fiona snapped: "So what was wrong with the person you were?" and quickly changed the subject. When Marion invited her mother to a ceremony at which she was to receive an academic award, Fiona declined without apparent regret, saying she had a doctor's appointment she couldn't change. By the time Marion started therapy, she had distanced from Fiona because she often felt furious after talking with her mother.

## Underground Anxieties

What was going on with Fiona? The notion that education was transforming her daughter into "a whole new person" probably scared her to death. What if this new person thought she was too good for her family? What if Marion began to feel ashamed of her mother? Perhaps, too, Fiona was struggling with envy, which would add to her ambivalence about her daughter's opportunities.

Deep in her heart, I imagine that Fiona was extremely proud of

Marion, and wanted Marion to embrace all the opportunities she'd never had for herself. But she also probably feared that if Marion became too different, she would lose her daughter. Or that Marion would lose her sense of family and where she came from. It's no small matter that Marion's educational opportunities would likely catapult her into a different social class from that of her parents.

As we worked together in therapy, Marion became more aware of the underground anxieties that fueled tensions between her and her mother. Eventually she felt ready to take a bold step forward. She invited her mother to her apartment for dinner, and as they relaxed afterward over coffee, Marion told her warmly:

"Mom, I'm so happy and grateful to be going to graduate school. This might sound ridiculous, but sometimes I'm afraid that if I get too much education, I'll lose my family. I worry that you'll love me less. And sometimes I feel that you disapprove of me for staying in school for so long. I wonder if you're proud of me or if you wish I had a family and a job and was settled down by now. What do you think about what I'm saying?"

Speaking to the real issues in this nonblaming way ("I'm afraid that if I get too much education, I'll lose my family") was Marion's first bold act of change. By speaking up this way, she helped ensure that Fiona's anxieties didn't stay underground, only to emerge later as potshots at Marion. But anxiety doesn't melt overnight. Fiona responded to Marion's disclosure with a dismissive "That makes no sense to me," and switched the subject to her garden.

## Staying Connected

Marion didn't take the conversation further that evening, because she knew it was not her mother's way to directly address an anxiety-provoking issue. But neither did she react defensively. She felt more empathic with her mother when she understood that her own professional development was felt as a threat, a potential loss, even an implicit criticism of Fiona's life and choices. She now saw her mother's obnoxious behaviors as the inevitable "Change back!" re-action that occurs in any family system when one person makes a shift that disrupts the relationship status quo.

Marion also watched her own tendency to distance from her family, and she avoided making comments that would unnecessarily raise Fiona's anxiety. For example, when she told her mother that education was making her "an entirely new person," it was pre-dictable that her mother's fears (and thus, her put-downs) would shoot sky-high. Instead Marion needed to make an extra effort to find common ground and stay connected to family members, and to value her mother's competence, even as she moved along in her own direction. Being a pioneer in one's family is never easy, and Marion's "fear of success" is apt to continue to haunt her if all she can do is distance from her mother or stay mad at her.

One Sunday afternoon, as they were having a cup of tea, Fiona surprised her daughter with a question. "Marion, so tell me what it is they are teaching you?" For a few seconds Marion's heart started racing again, reminding her of the day she landed in the emergency room. But after taking a few deep breaths to calm herself, she told her mother a little bit about her chosen field of art history. "Your grandmother was a good artist," Fiona responded, clearly warming to the subject. "You got this from my side of the family." Marion asked her mother more about her grandmother's art, which led to a conversation about Fiona's own abiding interest in quilting and other textile arts. Later Marion told me: "It was maybe the best conversation we've ever had."

Even if Fiona had not changed at all (and with your own par-ents, I encourage you to reduce your expectations to zero), Marion had acted and spoken courageously on her own behalf. She calmed her own anxious reactivity by taking her mother's comments less personally, and by understanding that there would always be a tug of war between her family's support for her growth and their fear of too much change. The bigger the change in any one generation, the higher the anxiety. Marion learned to pay attention both to her wish for personal growth and to her wish to preserve family togetherness.

## DON'T GO IN THE WATER

Whatever the particulars of your family background or current relationships, the key people in your life, past and present, may react anxiously to your moves forward, even when they genuinely encourage you.

An old folk poem goes:

*Mother may I go out and swim*
*Yes, my darling daughter,*
*Hang your clothes on the Hickory Limb*
*But don't go in the water.*

A parent may say, "Be successful!" but then ignore or undermine your success. "Go for it!" a partner or friend may cheer, but in parentheses whisper, "Don't go too far." Your husband may genuinely want you to get a prestigious promotion, but then react strongly if you start making more money or garner more status than he does. Or he may communicate, "Go for it, honey!" with the unspoken subtext, "as long as my life doesn't have to change." Or "as long as *you* don't change."

Even if we aren't on the receiving end of mixed messages, everyone has some anxiety about diving into new learning or new behaviors that will destabilize old beliefs and important relationships. As a psychotherapist, I help men and women to make courageous acts of change with the most difficult people in their lives—and in this arena I can tell you that fear is an equal opportunity employer. Because it's easier to do what we've done before, we generally will give ourselves reasons that we can't say or do something different, or shouldn't bother. It's only after we make a change that we are faced with the anxiety—our own and others'—that change evokes.

## COPING WITH COUNTERMOVES

The anxiety that accompanies change only *begins* when you take the first step of saying, asking, or doing something different that threatens the status quo. Next, the other person will make a "countermove" or "Change back!" maneuver to try to reinstate the old pattern and the old you. Fiona, for example, responded to Marion's move out in the world by withdrawing her interest and approval.

To review family systems theory 101, the process of change goes like this. One person begins to define a stronger, more independent self, or does something that violates the roles and rules of the system. Anxiety rises like steam. The opposition invariably goes like this:

1. "You are wrong," with volumes of evidence to support this.

2. "Change back and we will accept you again."

3. "If you don't change back, these are the consequences," which are then listed.

Countermoves can take any number of forms. You may be accused of disloyalty ("Do you know how much you hurt your father by visiting Uncle Charlie?") or selfish disregard for others ("You can't say that to Mom. It will kill her to know the truth!"). You may be accused of being misguided, crazy, or just plain wrong ("I know you can't really mean that"). The other person may threaten to withdraw or even terminate the relationship ("We can't be close if you feel that way"). Or they may sulk, argue, fight, gossip about you, or do whatever they do when they get anxious and threatened. Your kids will test you over and over to see if you "really mean it" when you tighten the structure.

A countermove can also take the form of other family members' refusal to recognize that you have indeed changed. Anxious systems are characterized by rigid rules, roles, and party lines ("Uncle Joe is a saint," "Aunt Mary is selfish") that may be written in stone. So if saintly Uncle Joe behaves unethically, that information will just be ignored, excused, rationalized, or disqualified. If selfish Aunt Mary acts with generosity, she may merely be seen as "manipulative." The failure to register and validate change is also a "Change back!" maneuver.

In whatever form they take, countermoves are simply the measure of the amount of anxiety in a system. It's not that the other person doesn't love you or want the best for you. Rather, the people who most depend on you to be a certain way may equate change with a potential threat or loss. Your job is not to prevent the countermove from happening, which is impossible. Nor is it to advise the other person not to react that way. Real courage requires you to sit with the anxiety that change evokes and stay on course when the countermoves start rolling in, as Marion did with Fiona.

Put simply, the challenge of change requires us to anticipate resistance from within and without—and to manage our own anxiety so that we can be our best selves when the other person, out of *his* anxiety, acts like a big jerk. When we gather our courage to move in the direction of greater authenticity and assertiveness, it would be nice if the other person would offer us enthusiastic approval and applause. But it rarely works that way.

## MY MOTHER/MY FATHER/MY SELF

I studied anxiety firsthand when I became interested in family systems theory and decided to change my position in a key triangle.
My long-term goal was to establish an emotionally close relationship with both my mother and my father. Before this time, my relationship with my mother had been at my father's expense, in that
he occupied an extreme outside position in the family. My mother
would not be off the plane for more than five minutes before she
would get me in a corner and whisper, "Let me tell you what your
father did now!"

In fact, fathers had occupied an outside position in my family
over several generations, while mothers and daughters were bound
together by unswerving loyalty. Before I became a student of family
systems theory, I simply saw my father as another inadequate man
on the family tree. I simply did not consider anything other than a
distant relationship with him.

Never did I so fully appreciate the power of resistance as when
I proceeded to move differently in this entrenched triangle. I vividly
recall my starting point—a memorable visit from my parents shortly
after the birth of my second son, Ben. My mother was washing
dishes in the kitchen, busily elaborating on my father's most recent
manifestations of immaturity and insensitivity. My father was entertaining my husband, Steve, in the living room, undoubtedly
making conspicuous displays of these same qualities. In the past, I
would have joined forces with my mom. This time was different.

I can still recall the terror in my bones as I told my mother that
I didn't want to talk about Dad anymore. With genuine warmth, I
went on to explain that the older I became, the more I realized that
I needed to have a relationship with both of my parents—and that
both she and my father were very important to me.

By the time I finished, my mother's anxiety had climbed sky-high. "You cannot know me," she responded with uncharacteristic coldness, "if you are unwilling to hear the truth about your father." I put my arm around her. "Mom," I said gently, "I want to get to know you from my relationship with you—and I want to get to know Dad from my relationship with Dad." She moved away from me. "Could you dry the dishes, please?" she coolly inquired.

And so it went. I had rehearsed the conversation in my head many times before my parents' arrival. Nonetheless, it felt like nothing short of treason. "I'm going to give her another cancer," I announced to my husband that evening. Earlier that week I had expressed a similar fear to my therapist/coach. "It will kill my mother if I say that." I knew such fantasies were irrational, but they spoke to my anxiety about losing my strong connection with my mother by going "too far" in changing my steps in the old dance.

My mother was not struck dead by my words, although she did have a predictably dramatic reaction, as she proceeded to test out whether I could be induced to reinstate the old pattern. The next morning, however, she appeared at the breakfast table looking cheerful and relaxed, having obviously enjoyed a good night's sleep. I had not slept well at all, and when morning came, I discovered large red splotches on my arms. This new and colorful symptom was a lesson in humility. My mother's resistance to change proved to be considerable—but less considerable, I confess, than my own.

This small slice of family life cannot do justice to the challenge of changing one's part in an entrenched family triangle. The process continues for many years—perhaps a lifetime—and involves getting derailed many times before one gets back on track and tries again. Over the years, however, I have been impressed not only by the powerful countermoves made by my own family members, but also by their remarkable flexibility about change, something I had not thought possible.

Change occurs slowly, and rightfully so. Making one small

change allows you to see how much anxiety you can sit with and how well you stay on track when countermoves come your way. It's the direction of change, not the speed of travel that matters. When people try to do too much too soon, they rev up so much anxiety that nothing changes at all.

## THE COSMIC COUNTERMOVE

Warning: The universe itself may send you a countermove if you make too bold a change! For example, you buy a house and the week you move in the dishwasher stops working and your car breaks down. You say to yourself, "Oh, no! It's a message that I never should have left my old apartment!" Well, I'm suggesting another way to look at it. It's merely the universe saying, yes, you are making a bold and courageous change! Here's my countermove! Prove your commitment to making this change!

To illustrate the cosmic countermove, let's return to my own family of origin story. When I first began to change my part in entrenched family patterns, I knew that such a task was not to be taken lightly. As a seasoned therapist myself, I understood the anxiety my changed behavior would evoke, and I fully anticipated encountering my own resistance to change as well as my family's "Change back!" maneuvers. But despite my intellectual sophistication, I was naïve and ill-prepared for my venture. No one had warned me about cosmic countermoves.

Here's the cosmic countermove in action in my case: Years after that memorable interaction with my mother in the kitchen, I visited my parents in Phoenix. I had just learned that my father, who prided himself on reaching the age of seventy-five without even a sniffle, had suffered a mild heart attack. This unexpected and unwelcome reminder of my father's mortality heightened my awareness that my parents were old and would not be around forever. During this visit I felt especially loving toward them both, and I was inspired to engage in yet another bold and courageous act of change.

It was this: I asked my father if he would make me a gift of an old prized Chinese print. I told him that I would frame it and give it a place of honor in my home. This request may not strike you as particularly daring, or even noteworthy. Nonetheless, the request and granting of this particular gift was a bold challenge to my family's long legacy of emotional distance between my father and me. Plus my mother collected art, donated generously to her daughters, and hated my father's taste.

My father carefully rolled the print into a cardboard tube so that I could hand-carry it safely on the airplane back to Kansas. His anxiety about this exchange was revealed only by the number of times he reminded me to keep it clean and frame it quickly, so that no harm would befall it.

At the airport his final words were spoken with affection, "Now don't get chicken schmaltz on that print, Harriet!" I had to smile at this reminder of my growing-up years in Brooklyn, and my father's chronic irritation at my habit of snacking while doing my homework, which sometimes led to "chicken schmaltz" finding its way onto my schoolwork.

I arrived home both pleased and anxious about this forbidden act of father-daughter closeness. Where could I keep the print until my schedule would permit a visit to the frame shop? I carefully removed it from the narrow cardboard tube and laid it flat on the carpeted floor of a remote attic room on the third floor of my large, old, Topeka home. Our entire third floor was reserved for guests, and this room was forbidden territory for the rest of the family. It was my private space, and it had long been my custom to sort out my manuscripts and documents on the floor there.

Three weeks later, after receiving an inquiry from my father about the print, I proceeded to retrieve it to bring to the frame shop. As I lifted the print from its place, I could not register or make sense of what my eyes saw. *The face of the print was crinkled and stained.* But this was not possible! I examined the papers on the floor surrounding it, and they were in perfect condition. I looked up at the ceiling directly above, half expecting to see a leak, but no leak was to be found. I stood staring at the print in stunned disbelief and recalled my father's final words to me at the airport: Had the heavens dripped chicken schmaltz on his prized print?

I rushed downstairs, print in hand, where a friend was drinking tea in the dining room. She was almost thirty years my senior and wise in the ways of the world.

"What is this?" I demanded of her, as I thrust the stained print under her nose. My friend looked and sniffed—and then made her diagnostic pronouncement. "It's cat urine," she said blandly.

And so it was. My sons had left the front door open, and one of the neighborhood cats that graced our front porch had made its way up two flights of stairs to find, and pee on, my father's beloved print. How can we understand such an action? Did he or she not have forty-five hundred square feet of floor on which to pee, to say nothing of the countless papers that were spread about the floor of our attic rooms? How can we fathom such a choice? And how could I explain it to my father?

It was in contemplation of this event that I published an article suggesting that the concept of the cosmic countermove should be added to the family systems literature. My colleagues thought the article was a hilarious piece of humor, but I was only partly kidding. I do believe there is a moral to my story. Dare you disturb the universe? Remember that changing an entrenched family pattern is only for the boldest among us. Do not begin the journey unless you are prepared to answer to the gods themselves.

As for my father, he took the news with surprisingly good humor. Perhaps—although I might have been wrong—I detected a tad of relief in his voice. Be it chicken schmaltz or cat pee, it is re-assuring to know that some things never change.

CHAPTER 7

# Your Anxious Workplace:

*Staying Calm and Clearheaded
in a Crazy Environment*

Work—it's a stressful business. That may not seem like big news to you, but the way anxiety plays out in the workplace is more complex and intriguing than you might imagine. For starters, it's not only individuals who get anxious. *Systems* get anxious, too. When a workplace is under stress (which is almost always), it will develop an anxiety disorder of its very own.

Are you part of a work organization, large or small? If so, you are part of an anxious system. "There is no other kind," observes organizational consultant Jeffrey Miller. Indeed, he suggests that if you happen to find yourself in an anxiety-free workplace, it won't be in business for long, so you should send out your résumé at once.

As Miller writes in *The Anxious Organization*, anxiety is "a force of nature, as elemental as wind and rain. It is what organizations are made of, and what makes them tick." Any system that doesn't register and respond to anxiety won't survive. Nor will you survive (or at least not well) if you don't know how to recognize the signs of an anxious workplace and figure out how to manage your anxiety at a personal level.

In these days of corporate corruption and collapse, ruthless downsizing and instant terminations, it may seem like a luxury to contemplate ways to identify and tame workplace anxiety. Many people live in fear of losing their jobs or not finding one to begin with. It's a wildly anxious time for economic survival. Nonetheless, most of us either work at some kind of job or are looking hard for one. As current or future members of a workplace, we must realize that our livelihoods will depend partly on how well we're able to size up and negotiate the anxieties of our particular organization.

If you are not currently part of a work system, don't skip this chapter. You can apply what you learn here to another system you belong to—your family, school, volunteer organization, church, synagogue, mosque, or government. We all operate in anxious systems a fair amount of the time. I'm reminded of novelist Mary Karr's definition of a dysfunctional family as "any family with more than one person in it." Likewise, a dysfunctional organization is any organization that has more than one person in it.

## GOING TO EXTREMES

If, like many people, you are part of an organization that is struggling with anxiety about resources and survival, you may know firsthand that it tends to behave just like a dysfunctional family under stress. *All* anxious systems have certain traits and characteristics in common.

As we've seen, anxiety causes a loss of objectivity and balance in individuals, pushing people to extremes. When anxiety and fear invade your workplace, your superiors will expect too little or too much, will underreact or overreact, be too authoritarian and involved or too hands-off and withdrawn. They will overfocus on your mistakes in an unhelpful way, or ignore your performance altogether. You will be denied the information and feedback necessary to do your job, or you will be given more information than you can possibly process and manage. Your organization will have little spirit for adventure and risk-taking, or it will plunge recklessly into high-risk ventures. There will be exaggerated calls to loyalty and sameness, or not enough cohesiveness and togetherness. Does any of this sound familiar?

Let me be clear: Anxiety is a good thing when it signals a problem and motivates a group to pull together to solve it effectively. Without anxiety, a system wouldn't register and respond to threats to its survival. But more frequently, this signal value of anxiety is lost. Instead, anxiety revs up everyone to "do something," even when the nature of the threat isn't clear. Even when it is clear, there may be no agreement about what to do. The lack of a coherent perspective and plan of action generate additional anxiety, which often turns into chronic, underground anxiety. This results in poorly thought-out behaviors, less objective thinking, and less creative problem solving. In addition, you can expect a steep decline in civility and cooperation among participants in the system.

You can't observe the actual anxiety in a system because anxiety is an invisible force that flows from one person (or department) to another. But you *can* observe the symptoms and signs of an anxious system, just as you can observe the symptoms and signs of your anxious self. *Observation* is the first step in changing your own anxiety-driven behaviors so that you can become more comfortable and effective at work.

## Is This Your Boss?

If you're in a chronically anxious (read, dysfunctional) system, your boss or supervisor will probably do what anxious people automatically do. When stress hits, she might angrily confront someone or go for the quick fix. She might give in to the impulse to "do something," like calling an emergency meeting or demanding that an employee meet a near-impossible deadline. Of course, any "solution" hatched in the overheated incubator of anxiety will almost surely be the wrong one.

Other typical anxiety-driven behaviors might prevail. Your boss might become fixated on the "hot spots" in the organization while ignoring the quieter problems that also need attention. He might participate in gossip, take sides, and form cliques or triangles. He might apply personnel policies in an arbitrary or partial manner, or announce ambitious new plans or initiatives—then suddenly abandon them. When employees got embroiled in seemingly unresolvable conflicts, he might overfocus on certain "difficult personalities" ("Bob is passive-aggressive") rather than staying task-oriented, gathering facts, and clarifying policy and procedures.

What else? Your anxious boss might fail to ask clarifying questions, state clear expectations, give direct feedback about performance, or listen well to the differing opinions of others. Instead, her communications might be vague, contradictory, mystifying, or dictatorial. Or she might try to make her employees feel like "one big happy family" by failing to take unpopular positions when need be, or by refusing to allow open expressions of dissent.

I'm not just making a laundry list of the regrettable qualities your lousy boss may have. We tend to think of an individual's behavior as reflecting fixed "personality characteristics." But people are capable of varying levels of competence, depending on their own level of stress and the level of anxiety in the system. If your boss were magically free of anxiety and stress, he or she might be-have with far more clarity and maturity.

But reality is reality. If your workplace is chronically anxious, your boss, as well as other people you interact with at work, may drive you crazy a good bit of the time. You will be vulnerable to absorbing high levels of anxiety yourself unless you know how to protect yourself by recognizing and modifying your own style of managing stress.

So put on your anthropologist hat and think of yourself as an ob-server of a fascinating culture. It is the culture of the anxious system—your workplace system. Keep in mind that all systems are anxious a good deal of the time, to one degree or another. Obviously, anxiety is highest when resources are scarce and the well-being or survival of your organization is threatened. But it's important to remember that *any* change can trigger anxiety in a system. So even when your work-place has abundant resources, you can count on the fact that your work system, like your family system, will be regularly hit with sources of stress from changes both inside and outside the organization.

## ANXIETY TRAVELS!

When stress hits your workplace, anxiety will zoom through the system as everyone tries to get rid of their own by dumping it on someone else. How you manage your own anxiety, no matter where you are in the work hierarchy, will either calm things down or further rev things up.

From a systems perspective, there are five styles of managing anxiety. These are the patterned ways we move under stress:

- Underfunctioning
- Overfunctioning

- Blaming

- Distancing

- Gossip, gossip, gossip

These behaviors are a good barometer of the level of anxiety in any work (or family) system. Of course, there are an infinite number of things that you might do to reduce your personal stress and get comfortable, like eating the bag of potato chips that's stashed in your desk or going for a walk around the block. But there are only five automatic patterned ways that we behave *in relationships* under stress.

Each of these styles of managing anxiety bring short-term comfort with a long-term cost, like eating potato chips. Your style of managing anxiety will interact with the other person's style of managing anxiety, generating increasingly high levels of tension. If you have an especially intense relationship with someone in your workplace, you know how hard it can be to wake up in the morning, put your clothes on, and go to work. Let's take a look at how anxiety travels, and how we can avoid absorbing too much of it ourselves—or passing it along to others.

## WHOSE ANXIETY ARE YOU CATCHING?

During my first job, I learned how quickly anxiety travels, and how easy it is to participate in a downward-spiraling process. Actually, I didn't learn a thing when I was in the system—except how miserable I was and how victimized I felt. It's hard to be objective when we're in the soup. Plus, I knew nothing about systems theory at the time and viewed everything as a matter of individual pathology—the *other* person's pathology, of course. I was riveted on who was right and what was true, rather than observing and modifying my style of managing anxiety and stress.

Here was my scenario:

SETTING: A large psychiatric hospital in San Francisco
PLAYERS (from the top down):
*Dr. Pattel,* director of the psychiatric hospital
*Dr. White,* chief psychologist (reports to Dr. Pattel) and my therapy supervisor
*Me,* psychology intern at the hospital
*Ms. Walters,* senior secretary
*Alice,* nineteen-year-old daughter of Dr. Pattel
*Plot:* Alice called me for psychotherapy. I agreed to see her. Anxiety cascades down the system, at the expense of everyone's functioning.

### SCENE I: FRIDAY AFTERNOON AT WORK
Alice called me at work and asked to see me in psychotherapy. She and I had been introduced at a party in Berkeley a week earlier. I had time available so I agreed to meet with her.

### SCENE II: SATURDAY AFTERNOON AT DR. PATTEL'S HOME
Alice told her father, Dr. Pattel, that she would be starting therapy with me next week. He became extremely anxious. Understandably, he wanted Alice to be seen by a senior therapist with more status and experience than I possessed. Also, he was not especially fond of me, which may have been why Alice chose me in the first place.

### SCENE III: SATURDAY EVENING PHONE CALL
Dr. Pattel phoned my supervisor, Dr. White. He angrily demanded to know why Dr. White had allowed this to happen. In fact, Dr. White knew nothing about the situation, because I planned to inform him during our supervision meeting the following Monday. Indeed, I had no inkling that agreeing to see Alice was a big deal

because I had permission to pick up appointments if I had open hours. In fact, I was flattered that Alice had chosen me as her therapist, and I naïvely thought that Dr. White would be pleased as well.

## SCENE IV: MONDAY MORNING AT WORK

I arrived at work Monday to find a memo in my mailbox from Dr. White, typed by Ms. Walters, the senior secretary, who sat at the front desk. Dr. White wrote that he was "dismayed and disappointed" that I had agreed to see Alice without consulting him and noted that my failure to talk with him before the weekend had put him in a bad light with Dr. Pattel. Dr. White said he wanted to meet with me "immediately" even though we had a scheduled supervision meeting that afternoon. The tone of the memo was stern and admonishing. I was flooded with anxiety.

## SCENE V: FROM BAD TO WORSE

Before I had even met with Alice for an initial appointment, the emotional climate surrounding the therapy process was anxious and emotionally intense. Dr. Pattel had passed his anxiety along to Dr. White, who in turn had passed it on to me.

The wisest course might have been to call Alice at this point and tell her that, unfortunately, I had been mistaken and I couldn't see her. In fact, she probably would have gotten better treatment outside of her father's hospital. But Dr. White informed me that he and Dr. Pattel had decided that I would see Alice, and that Dr. White would supervise my work with her very closely.

And so he did. What developed was an excruciating overfunctioning–underfunctioning dance. Dr. White micromanaged my work with Alice at the expense of paying attention to my work with other patients. As an inexperienced therapist, I was anxious to begin with, but under Dr. White's intense scrutiny, I had increasing difficulty reaching for my competence and drawing on my creativity and intuition in my work with Alice. I constantly feared saying the wrong thing to her, rather than simply viewing mistakes as an opportunity to learn. Whenever I met with Alice, I felt Dr. White's stern presence in the room. I'm quite sure Dr. White felt that Dr. Pattel was looking over his shoulder, too.

Several months into the treatment process, I forgot a therapy session with Alice. She sat in the waiting room in her father's hospital, while I was nowhere in sight. It was the first time I had ever spaced out on a therapy appointment, and I'm sure my anxiety (and tamped-down anger) contributed to my forgetting. To make matters worse, I had neglected to give my weekly schedule to the secretary, Ms. Walters, as I was supposed to. She didn't even know where to look for me.

Ms. Walters jumped into the fray by calling Dr. White and informing him that Alice had an appointment with me and I had gone AWOL. She added that I hadn't filled out my schedule, and mentioned that I often neglected to give her a completed schedule at the start of the week. While this was true, Ms. Walters had never spoken to me directly about the problem. Dr. White's reaction was immediate and intense: *Everything* must be done to locate me. Phones starting ringing throughout the hospital, but I was nowhere to be found. Even now, decades later, I recall exactly where I was during that hour. I was in a café down the street, happily eating a roast beef sandwich.

I walked back into a thrum of anxiety. There was a stack of memos and phone messages waiting for me, as well as disapproving looks from the secretaries. Dr. Pattel passed me in the hall with averted eyes and no greeting. Even before I took my coat off, several people told me that Dr. White was looking for me.

## SCENE VI: FROM WORSE TO WORSER

En route to Dr. White's office, my anxiety blossomed into anger. This was the first time I had forgotten a therapy appointment. I regretted it, but it was not a huge deal. I knew of other psychology interns, and even senior staff members, who had done the same. How could I function in this crazy goldfish bowl? I was enraged by the entire situation, including Ms. Walters's incendiary call to my supervisor, which was certainly not standard procedure.

I did exactly the wrong thing. I walked into Dr. White's office and began, "I'm sorry I forgot the appointment with Alice, but . . ." Then I proceeded to blame Dr. White for my situation, implying that he was partly responsible for my spacing out on the session, because how could I possibly do good work with him breathing down my neck?

I believe I put it more tactfully than that, but as you might imagine, this conversation did not go well. Dr. White responded to my defensiveness and blaming by becoming more defensive and blaming himself. He told me that even the secretaries found me difficult and that my failure to fill out my weekly schedule reflected "a narcissistic sense of entitlement." He noted that my poor attitude would be reflected in my written evaluation. This infuriated me further and made me sorry I had ever agreed to see Alice.

I thought things couldn't get any worse, but I was wrong. I was late for my next therapy session with Alice! I took a phone call five minutes before the appointment and didn't watch the clock. Ah, the power of the unconscious! Ms. Walters knew I was in my office, and she could have simply knocked on my door or buzzed me. Instead she called Dr. White and announced that "Alice has been sitting in the waiting room for ten minutes while Harriet is on the phone." Dr. White banged on my office door, furious. "Why aren't you with Alice?" he barked. Awash in anxiety, I proceeded to do what anxious people do. I distanced, blamed, gossiped, and so forth.

## The Postmortem

Only later did I understand that all the players in this drama had the same goals, which were to provide Alice with good therapy, and to get comfortable themselves. In anxious situations, people rarely have bad intentions. In my workplace, everyone was trying to make a difficult situation better, but responded in his or her automatic, patterned way of managing anxiety. Unwittingly, everyone made it worse.

Perhaps you sympathize with one person more than another. At the time, I sympathized entirely with myself and blamed everyone else. It's easier to blame others than to observe how anxiety travels through a system and develop a plan to modify one's own anxiety-binding behaviors. Let's consider how all the players could have managed their anxiety more functionally—from the top down.

### Dr. Pattel

The anxiety could have been contained right here. Dr. Pattel had the authority to tell Dr. White that I was not to see Alice. Or, if he did want me to see his daughter in therapy, it was not constructive for Dr. Pattel to make an intense call to Dr. White at home over the weekend. Dr. Pattel could have waited until Monday and calmly communicated that he was concerned about my inexperience, but confident that Dr. White would do a good job supervising me. Then he could have bowed out of the process. This would have helped to create a calmer emotional climate, which ultimately would have given the therapy the best chance of succeeding.

## Dr. White

Dr. White could have contained the anxiety that Dr. Pattel passed on to him, rather than passing it on down the pike. When Dr. Pattel called him on Saturday, Dr. White could have stayed factual and calm. ("I'll check with Harriet on Monday, since I didn't know about this. Would you like me to tell her to refer Alice to another therapist?")

The critical memo that Dr. White left in my mailbox Monday morning also drove the intensity higher. He could have waited to talk to me during our regular supervision hour later that day. He might have said lightly, "You know, Harriet, what you did was totally understandable, since the policy is that you can accept patients who call you directly when you have open hours. But since Alice is the daughter of the head of the department, you should have checked it out with me before agreeing to see her." Obviously, I would be more likely to be able to hear constructive criticism if it was delivered calmly and respectfully.

Dr. White also could have gotten a grip on his own pattern of overfunctioning under stress. By focusing on me as "the problem" in an intense and worried way, he only made the situation worse. Ditto for his supervising me too closely, and focusing more on my incompetence than on my competence. Also, his comment on my personality ("You have a narcissistic sense of entitlement") was a form of blaming and one-upmanship that only drove the anxiety higher. It would have been better if he had stayed with facts and expectations. ("Giving your schedule to Ms. Walters each week is part of your job and you need to do it.")

## Ms. Walters

Ms. Walters escalated the anxiety further by overstepping boundaries. It was not standard procedure for a secretary to call a therapist's supervisor about a late or missed appointment. If she had first brought my problematic behavior to my attention, her next step in the organization system would have been to go to my supervisor. But she had never talked directly to me, whether the issue was Alice sitting in the waiting room or my failure to give her my schedule.

When we talk *about* a person being a problem, rather than directly *to* the person, we add to the underground anxiety and make it harder for the talked-about person to behave with confidence and competence.

## My Part in the Dance

I did most of the automatic things we do under stress. I underfunctioned, blamed, distanced, and gossiped—the whole works! Let's take a closer look at the five styles of managing anxiety, with an eye toward learning more about the patterned ways we move under stress.

## THE FIVE STYLES OF MANAGING ANXIETY

### Underfunctioning

My sibling position (the younger sister of a sister) primed me for *underfunctioning*—doing too little. You don't need to be a youngest child to underfunction. But youngests are naturals, just as eldests are natural overfunctioners and can become control freaks under stress.

Underfunctioning in the workplace can take many forms. You may not meet the requirements of the job. Or you may be quite competent, but present yourself in a manner that invites people to see you as spacey, immature, or irresponsible. You may project an image of helplessness and vulnerability, inviting others to take over for you. You may do brilliant work, but underfunction in a specified area, such as not doing your paperwork, meeting deadlines, or showing up for meetings on time.

In the youngest child's quest to be a creative and charming free spirit, she may underestimate the importance of following rules, respecting hierarchies, and attending to the more tedious requirements of the job. Youngests tend to be very critical of authority, and quite certain they will do a better job—but may drop leadership like a hot potato if it's actually offered to them. Youngests may also underfunction by sharing personal information at work before taking enough time to test out the maturity level of the individuals they take into their confidence.

I needed to get a grip on underfunctioning. It was my responsibility to figure out how I could do my best work with Alice. It was also my responsibility to meet all the requirements of my job, including filling out my weekly schedule and getting it to Ms. Walters in a timely fashion. If I had a lot of status, perhaps I could have gotten away with underfunctioning around the edges. But as a junior person, I needed to do everything required of me, rather than thinking that my talent for the "real work" of psychology excused me from the parts of the job I disliked.

Here are the lessons I learned, if not on the job, then after the job.

## Lesson #1: Take Responsibility

Meet all the requirements of your job before asking for a special project or privilege. Abide by the rules. Many details of the job may seem trivial or tedious to you, like meeting all your paperwork deadlines or returning from lunch on time. If they are important to your boss or supervisor, do them.

Underfunctioners often get labeled "a problem." So in addition to meeting your job requirements, be cautious about sharing personal problems and other sensitive information in your work setting. Take time to assess who is mature, kind, trustworthy, and discreet— and who is not.

## Blaming

It has always been my strength to speak openly and directly to authority when I am angry about injustice. But the productive use of anger is different from nonproductive blaming that gets nowhere or even makes things worse. Dr. White was already anxious himself, and my attempts to be "open" with him, especially when I had no consideration for such matters as timing and tact, only raised the intensity higher.

Instead, I should have focused on my part of the problem and figured out how I could lower the negative intensity between us. For example, it didn't help matters when I criticized Dr. White for supervising my work with Alice too closely. Instead, I might have said, "Dr. White, I appreciate your help with Alice, but I feel as though I'm neglecting some of my other patients." (This was true.) "I need to use this supervision hour to talk about Charles. I'm really stuck in my work with him right now and I need your perspective." That way, I would have related to his competence and I would not have been seen as a blamer and complainer.

Likewise, I could have found a diplomatic way to talk about my anxiety working with a VIP under such close supervision, without implying that Dr. White was responsible for my feelings and behaviors. For example, "Dr. White, I appreciate your help with Alice but it also makes me anxious to know that my work in this case is being watched so closely. Do you have any advice on how I could deal with this anxiety, or work more collaboratively with you on helping Alice?"

## *Lesson #2: Think It Through*

Blaming is an automatic response to anxiety. You overfocus on what the other person is doing to you (or not doing for you) and underfocus on your own creative options to change your part in the problem. You lose your capacity to see two sides of a problem, or better yet, six or seven sides.

Your anger may be totally legitimate, but as my friend Marianne Ault-Riché says, "It is when the other person is being the biggest jerk that you are called upon to be your most mature self." When anxiety is high, it's far more important to be strategic than spontaneous. When an organization is under stress, any one individual can easily become a candidate for the position of "problem employee." Don't raise your hand and volunteer for the job by getting seen as a blamer or complainer.

While clear and direct communication is always a good move, people confuse "honesty" and "clarity" with blaming ("I told my boss he was sexist and threatened by strong women"). Blaming is the easiest way to ruin your career. It's surprising how many people blame when it *never* benefits the blamer. If you observe the best employees or bosses, they don't blame, they just talk about the facts of what happened with another person.

When you're feeling angry or intense, take time out to calm down. Then consider what you want to accomplish and how you can state your different views without getting critical or defensive yourself.

## Distancing

When anxiety hits, we all withdraw from the people we find difficult. When I got sufficiently uncomfortable, I said to myself, "Dr. White is so impossible that I am just going to stay in my office, shut the door, and speak to him only when absolutely necessary in our weekly supervision meetings." And "Ms. Walters and the other secretaries are gossiping about me and I'm going to avoid them, too." And "Dr. Pattel should be staying the hell out of this therapy process, and I don't want to see his face."

So what's wrong with that? As a family therapist friend says, "Thank God for distance and cutoff!" We *do* need to protect ourselves when the feelings evoked by connecting are unmanageable or simply too painful. Withdrawal does relieve anxiety and intensity. The flight response (like the fight response) is wired into us for good reason.

Here's the problem: Other people's misperceptions about you will only harden if you avoid showing your face. The more you distance from people in your work group, the more you will become the target of other people's inaccurate perceptions and gossip. You will carry more underground tension in the long run if you avoid the short-term anxiety that is evoked by making some contact.

### Lesson # 3: Hang Out Rather Than Hide Out

Show up at events, office parties, and informal gatherings around the coffeepot. Look people in the eye, smile, and say hello. Use humor, bantering, and small talk to lower the tension with difficult people. Try to move *toward* the person who is most critical of you, show some interest in his work and ideas, and give the difficult people credit for good qualities they have.

Temporary distance is crucial, especially when we need to calm down, think, and make a plan. Just don't let it get entrenched. Plus, if you don't make regular contact and engage in bantering and small talk during calm times, there's no chance you'll be heard when you try to address a controversial issue.

• • •

*Emotional distancing* is a subset of distancing: You may show up bodily, but withdraw emotionally. You fail to say what you really think about important issues. You silence yourself because you don't want to make waves, criticize, or draw negative attention to yourself. Or maybe you've just "given up." You may sit in meetings entertaining your own private fantasies. Or you may try to pay attention, but you're not an authentically engaged participant.

Emotional distancing isn't my automatic style, or at least not my first line of defense. I tend to overtalk hot issues when I'm anxious, rather than avoiding them. But I have been in work settings where emotional distance prevails—and boredom and flatness result. Lifelessness; disengagement; fatigue; "burnout"; the loss of spontaneity, creativity, and vitality are the hallmarks of a system where silence and secrecy prevail and anxiety is managed primarily by emotional distancing.

## Lesson #4: Stay Present and Be Direct

That doesn't mean you need to speak to every irritation that comes along. My automatic tendency to confront every injustice in the workplace has often been unproductive. It's an act of maturity to choose your battles and let other things go. When an issue is important to you, you need to be able to ask clear questions, say what you think and believe, and clarify where you stand. But choosing your battles is especially important because anyone who tries to change too much of the organization is seen as a "problem person."

## Gossip! Gossip! Gossip!

What is "gossip"? We gossip when we talk *about* someone, rather than directly *to* him. Two people move closer to each other at the expense of the gossiped-about party, who is focused on in a critical or worried way. You can measure the amount of anxiety in any system by the amount of gossip going on.

When things got intense with Dr. White, I gossiped away! For example, I tried to get some sympathy from a bright young psychiatrist by badmouthing Dr. White and telling her how impossible he was. I described him as "a nasty little ferret," zealously nosing around to uproot my imperfections. At first she was sympathetic. But Dr. White also supervised her, and she needed to have a good relationship with him. She soon became Dr. White's "golden girl" and distanced from me. As the outsider in a triangle I had helped to create, I found that my anxiety increased further.

Can it ever be useful to involve a third party? Of course. When I was having trouble with Dr. White, it would have been helpful for me to seek out a wise, clearheaded person for advice about better managing my relationship with him. But I wasn't looking for helpful coaching, which requires a focus on the self. I was looking for an ally—a perfectly normal human impulse. So I grabbed anyone I thought might be sympathetic.

The higher my anxiety, the more I wanted to corner everyone and say, "Let me tell you what that horrid, intrusive little ferret is doing *now*!" That would have been fine to do with my husband or best friends. But talking about Dr. White to others in the workplace, and especially to the young psychiatrist who needed to have a good relationship with him, was unwise. A good rule about gossip is to try not to say anything that you wouldn't want to be overheard.

## Lesson #5: Be Straightforward

When you are having a problem with someone at work, talk directly to that person. If you're angry with Gregory, don't complain about Gregory to Sue, especially if Sue needs to have a viable work relationship with him. At best, gossiping can only work short-term. If you stop Sue in the hallway to spout off about Gregory and she responds sympathetically, your anxiety may diminish. Letting off steam this way may help you to calm down and manage things with Gregory in a better way. We participate in this kind of transient gossip all the time, sometimes with no harm done.

Of course, it's better to say, "Sue, I'm having some trouble working with Gregory. Do you have any advice on what I can do to make this easier?" When you make gossiping a habit, it can backfire big-time. If you keep up the negative focus on Gregory, Sue may become more distant from Gregory or more reactive to him. If Gregory is underfunctioning, he will have to work even harder to gain competence if he's the subject of gossip. Or if Sue begins to like and respect Gregory, she may begin to distance from *you*. Gossip creates insiders and outsiders. It makes it more difficult for all parties to resolve the issues between them and to feel competent and included.

## Overfunctioning

Overfunctioning—doing too much—takes several forms. It's the natural province of firstborns, who tend to think they know what's best not only for themselves but for everyone else on the planet. Dr. White overfunctioned in typical firstborn fashion, supervising my work too closely and failing to recognize that his hypervigilance only increased my anxiety.

Overfunctioning was the one thing I did *not* do in my first workplace. But I did my share of it over the course of my long career at the Menninger Clinic. My particular "youngest" style of overfunctioning was to act as though I had the truth of the universe and to zealously try to convince my misguided colleagues of the error of their ways. I jumped into the center of every hot issue, overtalking my point even after it was clear that my listeners had had enough. The combination of my overfunctioning (trying to change, educate, and reform my colleagues) and underfunctioning (losing forms under piles on my desk, ignoring administrative protocol) did not endear me to my superiors. In fact, I was told I had the "largest personnel file" of any psychologist in the history of the institution. While my friend Stephanie considers this distinction "a shiny badge of honor," it caused me considerable pain to be the target of negative focus.

## Lesson #6: Know When to Stop

To begin to let go of overfunctioning, it may help to consider how your sibling position may influence your style.

If you are the older sister of a sister, you may overfunction in a manner that gives you the reputation of being a bossy control freak.

If you're an older brother (or the first male in your sibling group), you're in luck. Your overfunctioning may lead you to be seen as a "natural leader" and a person who knows how to take charge. (If you think this might be sexist, you're right.)

If you're the older sister of a brother, you won't ruffle feathers. But in your unassuming, tactful way of assuming leadership, others may overlook your competence and contributions.

If you're a middle sibling, you may be seen as a "good team player." Your style of overfunctioning may involve taking on extra work and responsibilities, while ignoring your own career goals or failing to formulate them in the first place.

If you are a middle sister with brothers, you may be particularly dutiful, sensitive to the needs of others, as well as conflict-avoidant. You may also be overly tolerant of the underfunctioning of others, and overfunction by picking up slack for others who screw up or slack off.

Overfunctioning youngests, as I said earlier, can act like bossy know-it-alls but are typically more interested in feeling included, appreciated, and understood, than in assuming leadership.

Of course, a person in any sibling position can adopt any or all of the five styles in the same work context—and even on the same day. All of these styles are normal and ordinary ways of navigating relationships under stress. The higher the anxiety, the more we "overdo" these behaviors. This contributes to more anxious reactivity. So we need to calm down, think clearly, and modify our own style of navigating relationships under stress.

## THINK SYSTEMS!

When my workplace drama (still painful after all these years) unfolded, I had no idea how to "think systems." To understand anxiety from a systems perspective, keep these key points in mind:

1. Anxiety is a characteristic of human systems, not something that exists only in the individuals who comprise the group.

2. Everyone in a system is connected to everyone else. That means you will always be reacting to how other people manage their anxiety, just as they will always be reacting to how you manage your anxiety.

3. Anxiety rarely stays contained within one or two individuals. Rather, it zooms through a system at high speed, gathering steam at every point along the way.

4. Anxiety is contagious. Intensity and reactivity only breed more of the same.

5. Calm is also contagious. Nothing is more important than getting a grip on your own reactivity.

In an anxious system, someone will always be dumping his or her anxiety on you. It's an automatic process, not anybody's villainous plan. Keep in mind that blaming, gossip, distancing, underfunctioning, and overfunctioning are normal expressions of anxiety. As you learn to recognize the signs of an anxious system, you will begin to stop taking things so personally and start observing people's automatic style of managing anxiety—your own included. If you can learn to think in terms of anxious systems, you will understand that anxiety makes nice people do obnoxious things. Or, as Jeffrey Miller puts it in his gem of a book, *The Anxious Organization*, "anxiety makes smart organizations do stupid things."

The challenge is always to observe, think about, and modify your part in the relational impasses that are causing you pain. The only part of the system you can change is your own reaction to anxiety. You can learn to let other people's anxiety float by you, and to pass on less anxiety than you receive. When we can transmit less intensity than we receive in the systems we belong to, we are not only moving in the direction of calming things down. We are also doing what the world desperately needs: creating a more peaceable, openhearted place to live.

## WHAT ANXIETIES DO *YOU* BRING TO WORK?

Your workplace is an anxious system that will pass anxiety along to you. But you also bring your personal anxieties to the workplace. First, there are situational stresses that you currently face. If your house just flooded and your daughter's illness flared up, you won't be in a very calm place when you go to work.

Then there are emotionally loaded issues that you carry with you from your past, including your place in your family of origin. What meanings do success and failure have for you? How have your fears of succeeding and failing been influenced by your parents' hopes, fears, expectations, struggles, work histories, and unfulfilled longings? You may come from a family where it was important to dazzle and shine. Or, by contrast, your parents may have considered it sinful to "have a swelled head" or to draw attention to the fact that it was you who hit the winning home run. You may be especially anxious about being unrecognized, or you may prefer invisibility and fear hurting others if you're not perpetually dimming your lights.

You will also have particular emotional triggers that get activated at work, depending on your experience growing up in your family. For example, your past may prime you to be especially reactive to being unappreciated, or feeling like "the outsider," or incurring other people's anger and disapproval. Or your emotional trigger may be the thought of being laughed at. You don't necessarily need to go into therapy and root around in your past to explore all the factors that evoke your anxiety in the world of work. But you do need to learn how to observe the five styles of managing anxiety in yourself and others. When stress is high you will automatically fall back on one or more of the five styles—and so will everyone around you.

Most important, you need to know that you can survive without a particular job, if need be. You must be prepared to leave. Many people feel they can't live without their jobs, but when they must, most manage to find a way to survive, and even to generate creative new options they never knew existed. If you're convinced you can't live without your job, then you can't really act on your principles, say what you think and feel, and maintain a clear bottom line. You will be vulnerable to anxiety, depression, and a host of stress-related physical ailments—all symptoms of helplessness. By contrast, when you recognize that you will ultimately survive without any *particular* job, you gain enormous power.

## A CAVEAT: DON'T CONFUSE WORK AND FAMILY!

For the most part, work systems and family systems operate in pretty much the same way. That said, never confuse your workplace with your family! There is one important difference. The family you grew up in might have been pretty crazy, but when financially hard times hit they probably didn't put you out on the street to fend for yourself. It is rare for a parent to put a memo on a child's desk, saying: "You've been with us for ten years, and you've always been a loyal family member, but money is scarce now, so we have to terminate you. Please have your belongings cleared out by 3 P.M. Our very best wishes for your future." A work system will do just that.

Sometimes a workplace will pretend it's a family. If an organization is thriving economically and does not feel threatened, it can pay a great deal of attention to your professional goals and job satisfaction. My organization claimed to be "family" when it saw itself as having unlimited resources and a future that stretched out forever. But as a family systems therapist reminds me, organizations live, sicken, and die just like people do. When survival anxiety is high, you will discover just how expendable you are. In fact, your "work family" may treat you in such an insensitive and uncaring manner that it will take your breath away.

I say this not to demoralize you, but rather to encourage you to keep your expectations realistic and your options open. The primary goal of a work organization is to ensure its own economic viability. Unlike a family, it does not exist to nurture your growth, offer you intimacy, or make you happy, although it's wonderful when those things happen. But work is work. Family is family. Don't confuse them—and you'll have one less thing to be anxious about.

# CHAPTER 8

# The Secret Power of Shame

Our fears may be dinner table conversation, but the shame that lurks beneath them may be a secret we keep even from ourselves. For example, a woman told me in an initial therapy session that she was afraid of talking in front of groups, something her job frequently required. She also avoided travel and taking on new challenges at work. It took a while for her to uncover the shame that fueled the engine of fear and apprehension the belief that if she put herself in unfamiliar situations, she would be seen for what she truly was—inferior, ridiculous, flawed, and fraudulent in some essential way.

We don't speak openly about shame—because we're ashamed to. My mother-in-law, Kathleen, told me that sitting among her family one evening, she posed this question to the group: "If you left the room, what would be the very worst thing that the rest of us might say about you—the thing that would hurt the most?" Her provocative question struck me as an invitation to share one's shame.

Everyone offered an answer ("the worst thing would be that I was boring"), but I wonder how truthfully. What we truly believe is most shameful about us—that part of the self that feels deeply and horribly *wrong*—is usually too shameful to talk about. Most of us will resist even thinking too long about the question Kathleen asked.

Shame is a profoundly debilitating emotion. No one wants to talk about it. When was the last time you opened up a frank conversation about your shame? Shame, by its very nature, makes us want to hide. Even *other* people's shame may make us avert our eyes.

Shame acts as a steady call to silence, inaction, and hiding. A part of us is flawed and should not be seen. It may be a physical part: hips, thighs, vulva, feet, stomach, a missing breast, skin color. It may be a nonphysical part: the needy part, the weak part, the loud part, the part that wants to dazzle and shine and be the center of attention, the part that takes up "too much" space—or not enough.

Shame drives the fear of not being good enough. You may carry shame around with you all the time, but be aware of it for only brief moments. You can learn to feel shame about anything that is real about you—your shape, your accent, your financial situation, your wrinkles, your size, your illness, your infertility, how you spend your day.

## WHAT IS SHAME?

Try to recall the last time you felt ashamed. What did you actually experience? Perhaps you flushed slightly, lowered your eyes, and tried to avoid the gaze of others. Maybe you wanted to disappear, or wash yourself clean. It's hard to describe what shame *feels* like, because this particular emotion doesn't always provide us with clear, unmistakable, in-the-body signals, as does a jolt of fear or a wave of anxiety.

For many people, shame has a kind of nightmarish quality, drenched in the horror of exposure. My friend Emily put it this way:

> It's like you are going along, passing in the world, and then, oh my God, your defects are on display in this painful way. Like there is a fundamental flaw that suddenly you can't keep hidden. It's very visceral for me, like a yuk, poisoned feeling.

This is as good a description of shame as any I've heard. Shame is primarily a "social emotion," meaning it usually requires someone to be ashamed in front of. Even when we feel shame all by ourselves, we can conjure up an audience of individuals who look at us with disgust, disapproval, or pity.

Shame isolates us, separating us from others and from our shared humanity. We may gather strength from joining together in collective anger, grief, or fear. But few of us come together in "collective shame." Shame makes us want to draw inward, fold ourselves up, and hide. As psychologist Judith Jordon notes, shame removes us from the flow of human connection.

## Shame vs. Embarrassment

Over coffee with friends recently, the conversation turned to embarrassing moments. The story I told involved an extra pair of underpants creeping out one leg of my jeans and onto a busy street in Lawrence, Kansas, where I was strolling with my husband. I reviewed my options: Should I back up and retrieve them from the sidewalk? Or should I just keep walking, as if someone *else's* underwear had magically parachuted down on Massachusetts Street?

This very incident had happened to me twice before. I take my jeans and underpants off in one motion, and when I put my jeans back on the next day, I sometimes don't notice that yesterday's underwear is stuck in one of the pants legs, and will work its way south—and eventually out into the sunlight. When this has happened, I have felt embarrassed, but not ashamed. What's the difference?

Both embarrassment and shame are social emotions, linked to how we think we appear to others. But embarrassment is much lighter than shame. We don't equate the source of our embarrassment with an essential flaw in our personhood. In the case of the wandering underwear, my attitude was: Okay, I would prefer not to see my underpants on the sidewalk, but it's no huge deal. It could have happened to anyone who gets undressed as quickly and impatiently as I do. Or maybe I'm a big klutz, the biggest klutz I know, but hey, we all have our quirks. I know that life has constant reminders, far more serious than runaway underpants, that we're all flawed, imperfect human beings. Later the incident will become a funny story, part of a conversation with my friends where we are laughing hysterically about our embarrassing moments.

But what if the same incident has a different meaning to me? What if I respond to the sight of my underwear on the sidewalk by feeling awful and set apart? I might say to myself, "No one else would do such a stupid, tacky thing. What's wrong with me?" I feel blemished in some essential and horrible way. That's shame.

## Shame vs. Guilt

You can feel guilty and ashamed at the same time. A friend tells me of the guilt she felt as a child for masturbating and the equally terrible shame she felt when her mother walked in on the act. "I know what you're doing," she said sternly. "Don't *ever* do that again." My friend felt fear, too, as a good Catholic girl now en route to eternal damnation.

You can probably recall incidents in your own life when shame and guilt came together as one. But shame and guilt are distinctly different emotions. Guilt is what we feel when we behave in a way that violates our core values and beliefs—assuming, of course, that our conscience is in good working order. The experience of guilt is usually tied to specific behaviors that we're not especially proud of, like betraying a friend's confidence, or hurting someone in the name of honesty.

It's important to point out here that not all guilt is healthy. Some of our "core values and beliefs" have been transmitted to us by the culture for the purpose of holding us in place. Most women, especially if they are mothers, know all about the nonproductive guilt that can plague us if we act as anything less than a twenty-four-hour emotional service station to others.

But healthy guilt is a good thing. It helps us to regulate our behaviors by jolting us when we stray too far from being the decent, honest, responsible person we aim to be. When we injure someone with a snub or a put-down, we're apt to get zapped by healthy guilt. Our capacity to feel guilt preserves the dignity and integrity of the self and our relation to others.

Unlike guilt, the experience of shame is not tied to a specific behavior. Instead, it is linked to who we believe we are, deep down. We feel shame when we think we're too ugly, stupid, fat, mentally ill, needy, or incompetent to be worthy of receiving love or even walking around on the planet, using up valuable oxygen. Shame feeds the conviction that another person couldn't possibly love or respect us if he or she really knew the whole, pitiful, God-awful truth about us. Helen Block Lewis, perhaps the first psychologist to give shame its due, made this crucial distinction. Guilt is about *doing*. Shame is about *being*.

## THE SLAVE SALE AT P.S. 99

One of my worst experiences of shame took place in the fifth grade at Public School 99 in Brooklyn. The school was holding a "slave sale" in each classroom to raise money for the American Red Cross. Sound like a bad idea? I can only tell you that it was worse than you might imagine.

On the first day of this two-day fund-raising project, the boys stood before the class, and one by one, in alphabetical order, were auctioned off to the girls. The bidding began at one dollar and went up from there. I had saved my allowance for months for a boy named Donny, whom I had a wild crush on. When I won him, he was my "slave-for-a-day" and had to do my bidding. I was in heaven as I ordered him to sharpen my pencils, fetch my coat from the closet, and carry my books home from school.

The next day the girls lined up in front of the class and were auctioned off to the boys. My classmates were sold off at a fast clip. But when it was my turn, there were no takers at the one dollar starting price. After a silence that seemed like an eternity, the teacher asked,

"Do I hear fifty cents for Harriet?"

More silence.

"A quarter. Do I hear twenty-five cents?"

Silence and tittering.

I stared at my saddle shoes. I wanted to disappear.

"A dime?" A note of pleading had crept into the teacher's voice.

And then, more sternly, "Come on now, boys! Ten cents? Do I hear ten cents?"

Nobody stirred.

"Remember, boys, you can have more than one slave!"

Out of kindness, pity, or plain discomfort, Donny finally raised his hand. "I'll give five cents," he muttered. Later he said to me: "You don't have to be my slave. Just forget it."

I have never forgotten the experience of standing there on the "slave block," hot with shame and anxiety under the pitiless gaze of my classmates. I was skinny as a stick, and draped in a plaid jumper that was glaringly out of style. It was several sizes too big, one of my mother's thrift-store bargains. My mother always told me that I was "between sizes"—a concept I somehow never questioned. She believed in buying my clothing several sizes too large so that she could shorten the hem, and then lengthen it in subsequent years. Standing there in front of my appraising peers, I felt more than merely unattractive. I felt ugly, grotesque, light-years away from the possibility of being chosen.

It's easy to understand how shame can turn into social anxiety or a fear of social situations. If I had developed a school phobia, who would have blamed me? I pleaded with my mother not to go back to school after that day. She convinced me, somehow, that I could return and survive.

Telling the story today, I feel a different kind of shame—the shame that this terrible activity happened at all. Beyond the cruelty visited on "unchosen" children, how could my school so blithely mock and trivialize the horrors of slavery and its aftermath? It was the 1950s in Brooklyn, New York, not Selma, Alabama. Many progressive families in the school district, my own included, were active in the struggle against racial prejudice. Why did no teacher or parent speak up, resist? I can only imagine what the experience must have been like for the one African-American boy in our class. For him, which would have been worse—to have been passed over, or to have been chosen as a slave?

## SECONDHAND SHAME

Most of the time, our shame emanates from some imagined defect in ourselves. But as you probably know from your own experience, you can also feel shame about other people's traits, qualities, and behaviors, especially family members whom you believe reflect poorly on you. Let's look at the power of "secondhand shame" and how it operates.

## Paula's Story

Paula began therapy with me shortly after her sixteen-year-old son, Cliff, burned down a small building. He didn't intend to set the building on fire. He was, in his words, "just messing around." But he had acted impulsively and unwisely, and had caused a disaster. The event was front-page news in a small community where people had already been gossiping about what a loser this boy was, how he was turning into "a low-life," and how damaged Cliff had been by his parents' acrimonious divorce and "broken home."

Early in our work together, Paula told me how she had gone with a friend to a late-night movie and had run into a couple she hadn't met before. After introductions were made, the conversation turned to the stress of helping kids with their college applications. The woman turned to Paula and said, "Do you have children?" Paula froze. Looking at her feet, she murmured almost inaudibly: "One son."

"I feel tainted," she told me. "It's like the shame of my son is oozing onto me." She felt the same about her ex-husband, whom she described as an "unsavory character" who spent most of his free time in local bars. Her language—"oozing onto me"—captures the visceral sense that shame is poured onto us from the outside. And quite often, it is. The phrase "Shame on you!" was once the standard way to admonish a child.

## A Tangle of Emotions

Paula felt a deep sense of shame about Cliff's behavior and the resulting judgments about the quality of her mothering. But shame wasn't the only emotion that Paula experienced. She also felt anger at Cliff for screwing up and "causing" her to look bad. In addition, she felt fear and worry about his future, and guilt about her past parenting mistakes. Finally, she felt anger toward others whom she saw as judgmental, especially people in the community who labeled Cliff a "loser," as though his bad behaviors were the sum total of who he was. This confusing tangle of emotions made it even harder for Paula to approach the crisis with her son in a thoughtful, solution-oriented way.

Paula's anger was a healthy response toward the people who judged her by Cliff's behavior. A child's behavior is not a mirror reflecting back the good or bad job we have done. While Paula was responsible for her own actions, she was not responsible for her son's behavior, which she could influence, but not control. Paula herself was desperately overworked, and also lacked economic resources, supportive community ties, and necessary social services. Moreover, she had never received adequate help for Cliff's serious learning disabilities. Even if Paula had been lucky enough to have the privileges and resources that attend middle-class status, she would not have had the power to control her son's behavior.

Even though Paula was rightfully angered by the readiness of others to stand in judgment, she could not help but judge herself. After all, mothers are taught to take the primary responsibility for how a child "turns out." Shaming and blaming messages to mothers are everywhere in the culture, and Paula was not immune.

## Cutting Shame Down to Size

Shame breeds more shame. Whenever Paula went out in public she would keep her head down, averting her eyes. She preferred to stay home. But the more she withdrew, the larger her shame grew. She became anxious and even a bit paranoid about gossip, assuming, in the absence of facts, that she and Cliff remained everyone's favorite topic of conversation.

I doubted that this was so, because gossip gets old quickly and folks usually move on to new people to buzz about. But just as in the workplace, gossip *will* increase if the gossiped-about party begins to withdraw. In the absence of face-to-face contact, other people's fantasies and projections flourish. I told Paula that if she was concerned about gossip, she needed to stop hiding out and begin connecting with the very people she saw as critical. If she found it too hard to mention her son's difficulties, she could banter about the latest movie or the weather. Only through one-on-one contact would gossip and shame loosen their grip.

Paula rose to the occasion. She held her head high and forced herself to approach people, make eye contact, and chat. In response to the question, "How are you doing?" Paula responded "Fine, and you?" or "I'm hanging in there," or "Well, as you may know, this is a hard time for me." Her particular response depended on her mood at the time and who was doing the asking.

Sometimes Paula used humor to lighten things up. Once she found herself in a conversation with several women about one of their daughters who was featured in the newspaper for her outstanding academic achievements. Paula laughed and said lightly, "Well, if my son gets his picture in the paper again, I have a feeling it's not going to be because he's a National Merit Scholar!" The other women laughed with her, in a supportive, all-our-kids-are-trials kind of way. Then the mother of the superachieving girl asked Paula about how she and her son were doing.

## A Helpful Affirmation

Paula knew that the terrible shame she felt was not rational or deserved. "I did not set the fire," she said simply. "I did not burn the building down." Yet she *felt* as if she had. During one therapy session, she created an affirmation: "I am not my son. My son is not me." She wrote these words down on a piece of paper and kept it in her sock drawer, so she would see it every morning. To allow her body and mind to deeply absorb the truth of these words, she repeated her affirmation silently and out loud throughout the day.

Paula's message to herself spoke to the essential distinction between parental responsibility and control. We are responsible for our own behavior, including the responsibility to be the best parent we can be. We should be there for our child, seek help when we need it, and never give up on a son or daughter. But we do need to give up the magical fantasy that if we just do or say the right thing, we can determine how our child will think, feel, and behave. Nobody has that much control over another human being.

Step by step, Paula cut her shame down to size. She forced herself to show up. She practiced talking to others with a dignity she did not at first feel. She acted as though she had nothing to be ashamed of, and in the process of pretending, she moved closer to believing this truth. She began to ask other mothers, "Have you ever felt scared to death about your child?" and "Have you ever wished you could vaporize your child and make him disappear?" She began to hear from other desperate mothers about their high-maintenance, crazy-making kids. In the openness, lightness, and humor of friendship, Paula began to find her situation bearable. She was learning one of life's essential lessons: That what we believe is most shameful and unique about ourselves is often what is most human and universal.

## MY SON, MY SELF: MEL'S STORY

Let's consider one more example of secondhand shame in the parenting department. While Paula literally felt tainted with shame by her son, another therapy client, Mel, initially felt only worry and fear about Noah, his only child. Mel's experience of shame was more deeply hidden.

Mel described Noah as uncoordinated, "on the fat side," and the kid likely to be chosen last for any team sport. He added that despite these drawbacks, Noah appeared to be a happy kid who did fine in middle school and enjoyed hanging out with friends. So, I asked, what troubled him about Noah's weight and his lack of athleticism? In response, Mel expertly quoted the literature on childhood obesity, and told me how concerned he was about Noah's future health. More immediately, he worried that Noah's weight problem, combined with his glaring lack of athleticism, would set him up to be teased mercilessly by the other boys. His biggest fear, he told me, was that Noah would not fit in.

When Mel talked about Noah, he was at ease with the language of anxiety, worry, and fear. It took some time before Mel admitted to himself, and then to me, that he also felt a bit ashamed of his son's appearance. Mel was a senior partner in an engineering firm and told me that his partners had attractive, fit children. Mel noted that Noah was far from obese, but added, with barely disguised disgust, that his son had "sloppy fat." He described Noah's appearance as "soft and messy." He admitted feeling uncomfortable when he introduced his son to new people—and even trying to avoid it whenever possible. He also felt horribly guilty for feeling ashamed of his son.

## Looking Deeper

I asked Mel if he could recall feeling shame when he was growing up. At first, he couldn't relate. "I was good-looking, athletic, and popular," he assured me. "I was nothing like Noah." Only when I asked him about his dad's death, which happened when Mel was five, did he begin to recall a deep, pervasive experience of shame.

"I was the only kid in the school who had lost a father," Mel began. He told me about an incident in the first grade when the teacher asked the kids to draw a picture of everyone in the family. The teacher, ignorant of Mel's situation and apparently of life in general, asked Mel in front of the class why he had left his father out of the picture. "You don't have a *father*, you don't have a *father!*" a classmate had chanted later during recess. As the others chimed in, Mel fervently wished that everyone in his class had dead dads.

Once Mel connected with the word "shame" and his experience of it, he described shame as his constant childhood companion. He had felt deeply different from other kids whose families were "normal." During his youth in the 1960s, divorce was slowly losing its stigma, but the untimely death of a parent was still unspeakable. "I never knew when someone might ask me about my dad, or a teacher would have us make Father's Day cards, or our school or church would sponsor some father-son activity. I lived in fear of being found out."

Of course, Mel was far from alone in feeling shame about having a family that failed to replicate the mythical, picture-perfect family prescribed by the culture. I'm sure many of his classmates felt that their families were flawed for different reasons—some of them far more shameful than death. But back then, no one spoke about what went on in anybody else's house. Mel felt that he and his family were "passing," while other families were "regular."

## Newsweek Saves

One bright day in June, Mel nearly bounced into my office, a page from *Newsweek* in hand. He had brought a short piece by Adriana Gardella called "Living in the Shadow of a Lost Father," and Mel asked me to read it then and there, because he felt it described his own experience precisely.

Gardella went straight to the heart of the tremendous shame and loneliness she felt in a pre-*Oprah* world where even the word "cancer" was embarrassing to say out loud. With unapologetic candor, Gardella wrote about the humiliation and shame she felt when her father died from Hodgkin's disease at age thirty-six, which bought her an "exclusive membership in The Dead Dads Club." I noticed that Mel had underlined much of the article, including these words:

> And with something close to envy, I read about how kids whose parents died on September 11 gather at bereavement camps and learn they are not alone. They make memory boxes filled with mementos of their parents, and counselors guide them through "holidays and grief work-sheets." Fortunately, they're likely to be better prepared for Father's Day than I was.

Mel had found himself a long-distance role model who boldly exposed her shame to the light of day, right there in front of God and millions of readers. "She's my support group," Mel told me. "She says what I feel, exactly." He folded the article neatly and put it into his wallet, where perhaps he keeps it to this day.

Nothing can take the edge off fresh grief or magically heal the ongoing emotional aftermath of childhood loss. But realizing we are not alone can sometimes melt shame as quickly as Dorothy liquefied the Wicked Witch of the West with her bucket of water. Dissolving shame gave Mel his voice back. Shortly afterward Mel visited his mother in Florida and began a series of conversations with her about his dad, including how everyone in the family had reacted to the loss, and how Mel and his mom were feeling now.

## Talking to Noah

Mel's fear that his son Noah "wouldn't fit in" with the other kids illustrates the ways we confuse our children with ourselves. If Noah's body type was affecting his ability to fit in, he apparently had the emotional resources to handle it. It was Mel who had grown up feeling flawed and different. No resources were available back then to help Mel and his family cope with their grief and loss.

I encouraged Mel to talk openly to Noah about losing his father, including how ashamed, different, and alone he felt. He confessed to Noah that to this very day, he continues to feel that he lacks some "special knowledge" available to other men who grew up with dads. Before this conversation, Noah had seen his dad as "nothing but perfect," and he responded with genuine interest to his dad's self-disclosures. Their relationship became more relaxed, as Noah reaped the benefits of knowing a father who was real rather than ideal. It is a dilemma for a child to try to identify with a parent who seems close to perfect, just as it is a dilemma for a child to try to identify with a parent who can show hardly any competence at all.

Becoming aware of his shame, and talking with Noah about it, helped Mel to stop spilling his leftover feelings of inadequacy onto his son. He still felt embarrassed by Noah's appearance because he had absorbed our culture's teachings about what a boy should look like   lean and hard, not soft and pudgy. But this was embarrassment, not shame, and Mel learned to ignore it because he was no longer reacting out of his own vulnerability. He vowed he'd never again try to "hide" his son in social situations; instead he began to make a point of introducing Noah to his colleagues and friends. Whatever we seek to hide makes shame grow. Mel had had enough of that, and shame wasn't a legacy he wanted to pass on to his son.

By owning his own shame about his family, Mel also found that he could talk more freely to Noah about the issue of weight. He found creative ways to invite his son to talk about how he felt about his body. When Mel was carrying unexamined shame from his own past, he would have approached the issue of weight or "sloppiness" in a manner that would have conveyed disappointment and disapproval. He might have ended up shaming Noah, or at least shutting down the conversation by addressing the subject with an anxious, judgmental edge. He might have felt unable to open the conversation at all.

## THE PERSONAL IS POLITICAL

The extent to which you hide something important about yourself or another family member is a good barometer of shame. But while this urge to disappear or cover up feels terribly personal, the origins of shame are social and political. Mel grew up at a time when communities didn't deal openly with grief, and when there was one narrow picture of what a "regular" family should look like. Paula, for her part, felt shame because she had absorbed the cultural myth that a mother "causes" her child's behavior, and should be in control of the outcome. Shameful subjects in your own family may have included your dad's alcoholism or drug addiction, your brother's diagnosis of AIDS, your family history of manic-depressive illness, your immigrant mother's "broken" English. The particulars of what, and whom, gets shamed vary with time and place—but it's always *something*.

The amount of shame surrounding a particular issue—say, health, employment, sexuality, fat, fertility, or financial status—reflects both the personal meanings that you bring to an issue *and* the attitudes of the broader culture. Whatever is shamed, stigmatized, or misunderstood in the larger culture gets absorbed as someone's personal shame. The ignorance and prejudices of the culture will land smack in the middle of your most important relationships—which isn't fair to anybody. Shame breeds more shame as it locks a person, or a whole group of people, into silence and secrecy.

## A Lesson from Lena

Some people simply refuse to hide, even when the larger culture tries to shame and frighten them into silence. My friend Lena, for example, has done a terrific job of replacing shame with pride.

Lena, a lesbian activist, won't be complicitous for one moment with the disastrous prescription to act as though she should not exist. So she embraces her partner freely. They hold hands everywhere. When the checkout person in the supermarket recently asked her if she was married or had a boyfriend, she responded: "No, but I've been living with a woman for five years and we think of ourselves as married." No matter how anxious or vulnerable she feels, she refuses to be silent and thus "pass" as heterosexual. She knows that the greatest lies are often told in silence. She also knows, as the poet Adrienne Rich once said that when a woman tells the truth, she creates the space for more truth around her.

Is Lena ever afraid? Of course—and for good reason. High school students in her neighborhood have vandalized her car, a few people at work have snubbed her, and, most significantly, she almost lost custody of her son. She is no stranger to prejudice and hate. But she says she would no sooner go along with people's automatic assumptions that she's "straight" than would a black civil rights leader try to pass for white to avoid racism.

I'm grateful for the Lenas of the world who are totally and unapologetically out, whether the issue at hand is being gay or any other stigmatized or misunderstood trait or life circumstance. Visibility is a powerful shame buster. It builds pride and lifts self-esteem. It also starts a healthy chain reaction. Each time we dare to show the world who we truly are, it makes it a bit easier for others to step out of their stifling closets, too.

## The Real Challenge

The lesson of Lena's story is not that *you* should rush out and tell all. It may not be wise or safe to reveal particular facts about yourself. You need to make your own thoughtful choices about what to tell, how, when, and to whom. There is much to be said for being strategic and self-protective and for considering how much anxiety and shame you can manage when you predict a hostile or insensitive response.

It's obviously painful, risky, and exhausting to speak your own truths in a family, workplace, or community that fails to validate your experience, and would prefer to diminish, silence, and shame you and your kind. Not everyone can be like Lena. But we can all pay attention to whether we are helping others to feel valued and included or, alternatively, shamed and excluded.

To erase people is a terrible thing. We can do it—or have it done to us—without anybody intending harm. Once, on a plane trip, I spotted a famous runner, Jim Ryun, who later was elected to Congress. I asked him for an autograph for my younger son. He wrote, "To Ben: Run for Jesus." I was stunned by his assumptions, and equally stunned that I didn't gather the courage to tell him we were Jewish and to ask him for a different autograph. His assumption that everybody was just like him evoked in me a sudden shame about being different—"not regular."

There is no resting place in the challenge of creating a fair world where shame does not prevail. The higher the anxiety in any system, the less tolerance people have for inclusiveness, complexity, and difference. When you live in a culture of fear, you will likely want to huddle in a little family or village where everyone is just like you.

## AGE SHAME

We can all act in some small way to break the vicious circle of shame, silence, stigma, and secrecy. Consider the "don't ask, don't tell" policy that still holds sway in many circles when it comes to the subject of age.

Women have long been shamed for growing older—which is, after all, everyone's wish. Women have actually been taught to conceal their age, to joke and even lie about it, to treat it as a shameful little secret. "Oops," someone said, introducing me a while back. "I almost gave her age away!" I was heartened that no one in this audience laughed. Almost immediately I found a way to casually share my age with my listeners. If a light-skinned African-American person was introduced by joking, "Oops! I almost gave her race away!" we'd find the implications degrading rather than amusing.

What's interesting is that so many women still collude with the notion that if we are over a certain age, we shouldn't tell. We may fail to say proudly, or at least matter-of-factly, "I'm fifty-two" or "I'm seventy-one" or even "I'm thirty-seven." By staying silent, we perpetuate the notion that there is something shameful or lesser about growing older. We further shame and disempower ourselves, and all women, by agreeing that it is best to conceal the number of years we have been alive.

You get beyond shame by telling. Yes, there can be negative consequences. You may not get the job you applied for and deserve. Someone may stereotype you, or decide to not ask you on a date. But I guarantee you won't be censured, castigated, shunned, or imprisoned if you casually mention at the next party you attend that you'll turn fifty-one next month. So maybe you can start there.

I share my age with others much the same way I share the fact that I am a clinical psychologist, Jewish, married, and a Kansan. My age (fifty-eight as I write this and, I hope, older when you read it) is an identifying characteristic that allows others to locate me in time and history. Plus, getting older is my goal in life, the one upon which all my other goals rest.

You'll be in good company. On her seventy-fourth birthday, Maya Angelou said on the *Oprah Winfrey Show* that her breasts were in a race to see which could get to her waist first. The audience of women laughed, immediately and uproariously. They loved her combination of candor and humor because it didn't leave a whole lot of room for shame. Gloria Steinem got a similar response when she mentioned lightly in a keynote address that she has reached the age where she can't remember how she liked her eggs. You can probably think of other people you admire, like writer Anne Lamott, who use a kind of a self-deprecating humor that is actually empowering because it strips away something hidden for everyone to see and refuses to skulk around in silence and fear.

Considering the horribly shaming messages that people receive around issues of race, ethnicity, class, and sexual orientation, the matter of age may seem like a trivial one. But it's not. Colluding with the notion that older is lesser profoundly disempowers women, dissipating our energies in anxiety about our aging bodies, and convincing us that we are less valuable with each passing birthday. What would happen if all of us openly shared our ages without reticence or apology? What if, together, all women refused to treat age like a shameful secret or a "confession"? I believe the world would change tomorrow.

## A SINGLE SNOWFLAKE

The walls of my elementary school classroom, like most, were hung with posters carrying all manner of inspirational messages ("The best preparation for good work tomorrow is good work today!").

The quotes were trite but true, as inspirational messages tend to be. One in particular caught my fancy. "Nothing is more fragile than a single snowflake," it said. "But look what they can do when they stick together." I remember feeling suddenly excited about the promise of that message—and I still feel that way today. It's amazing what sticking together can do.

When it comes to fighting shame, sticking together is the most powerful force imaginable. The civil rights movement, the adoption reform movement, and the women's movement, just to name a few, illustrate how collective action can shrink the stigma that the dominant culture assigns to certain groups. As new, more positive meanings develop, individuals begin to replace silence and shame with pride and the ability to speak up on their own behalf. Lena would not be Lena had the gay and lesbian rights movement not worked tirelessly to change attitudes and laws.

While not all of us will choose to become social activists, each of us can do our part to create the conditions of safety for others to show up and be real. We can do this in small, everyday ways, by cultivating an attitude of respect, welcome, and openhearted curiosity about those who differ from us. There are many ways of sticking together—perhaps as many as there are snowflake designs. All forms of support, organized and ad hoc, collective and private, help to melt shame.

## BEING 109

Here's one more story to illustrate the personal and political nature of shame and how one woman slipped right out of its grip. Before I saw Elana in therapy, she had carried around two decades of shame about her "low IQ." When she was twelve, her father's friend, studying to be a clinical psychologist, had administered an intelligence quotient test. The results, as they were reported to her parents and then to Elana, stated that her IQ was in the "average range"—109, to be precise

Before "'fessing up" in therapy, as Elana put it, she had suffered in silence about "being 109." Whenever she had trouble learning or did poorly at something, she was convinced that her undistinguished IQ accounted for her difficulty. When she achieved success, she felt like a fraud whose underlying mediocrity might be discovered any minute. The number 109 haunted her. It was like a scarlet A branded to her chest, signifying "average."

Most people don't know their IQ scores, but many people secretly fear they're not as smart or competent as other people think they are and that eventually they will be discovered as impostors. Women often define "real intelligence" by male standards, or by whatever it is that someone else can do that they can't. Elana believed, for example, that her brother, a gifted mathematician, was brilliant, even though he didn't notice when someone in the room was upset. She believed that her own ability to grasp the complex nuances of social interactions made her a good teacher, but that her abilities came under the umbrella of "emotional intelligence"—a category she saw as separate from true intellectual ability.

## Knowledge Is Power

What helped Elana to get past her shame about a number that someone had assigned her twenty years earlier? First, she needed information to combat the myth that an IQ score reflects any objective truth about intellectual capacity. As a clinical psychologist who had administered IQ tests for much of my professional career, I could assure her that testing is useful in clarifying any number of important diagnostic questions, but not in measuring "general intelligence." Intelligence comprises more facets than we can ever begin to quantify, including such complex and invaluable skills as the capacity for friendship, for empathy, and for being perceptive, caring, alert, and emotionally present in the world. The richest and most critical aspects of intelligence cannot be assigned a number or ever be captured by a concept as arid as IQ.

Our definitions of intelligence are also defined by the historical context we happen to live in, and what qualities have importance for the particular community or tribe we belong to. For example, I happen to do work that is socially valued and economically rewarded in the mainstream culture. But some years back, when I joined some colleagues to lead a seminar with the Colorado Outward Bound Program, down the Yampa and Green rivers, I learned how it felt to be the least competent person in a work group. I had no outdoor skills and was slowest to learn them. I had difficulty mastering everything, from starting a fire, to tying our gear securely into the raft, to controlling my anxiety. Had it been an option, my colleagues surely would have voted me off the river.

As the week progressed, and the wilderness became my "real world," I understood that if I lived in that world on a daily basis, I would not see myself as a smart person. Had I been born in a different historical time, where the skills that were valued were the ones I didn't have, I would have to struggle so much harder to value myself. I might well have felt permanently inept and inferior, rather than just temporarily stupid in an area I could tell myself didn't really count.

Getting the facts can go a long way toward shrinking shame. For Elana, challenging false assumptions about IQ tests helped her to laugh and lighten up about how seriously she had taken a number. Gradually she was able to bring her once-shameful secret into the light of day. Elana began to tell her good friends about "the whole IQ schpiel." At her thirty-third birthday party, her best friends presented her with a T-shirt emblazoned with "109" in huge red numbers, which Elana put on during the party. She brought me a hilarious color photo of her friends gathered around her, making funny faces and pointing to the number on the T-shirt. "This is for you," she said, handing me the photo with a grin and a flourish. "You can put it in my chart."

# CHAPTER 9

# The Fear of the Mirror:

*Anxiety and Shame About Your Looks—
and Being Looked At*

When it comes to anxiety, fear, and shame, the body takes center stage—how it looks, how it functions, how it feels, how it has been cared for or violated, how it is changing, how long it will keep on keeping on. Each of us has a body, or more accurately, each of us *is* our body. No discussion of fear or shame can ignore the subject because the subject is us.

Of course, some people do have an entirely positive attitude. "I *love* the human body!" my friend Lorraine tells me. "It is so beautiful. And such a reliable source of joy!" It's *her* body Lorraine must be referring to. She's in her thirties, a camper, a rock climber, a hiker, and a tall, vigorous, lithe, muscular, gorgeous woman. I love watching her move. Illness and pain have never intervened in her good life. She says she has great sex. Lorraine is young and lucky— at least at the time of her enthusiastic proclamation.

Of course, the body *is* inarguably amazing. I recently appreciated this while watching the Cirque de Soleil acrobatic troupe perform in Las Vegas—a staggering display of athleticism, the body and spirit pushed beyond all imaginable limits. Even the ordinary, imperfect body that most of us have is miraculous in its complexity and functioning, even in illness and disability.

But the body is not always beautiful or a source of joy. And it is definitely not reliable. A colleague who is decades older than my friend Lorraine puts it well: "The body is no place to live in."

## THE SHAPE WE'RE IN: LESSONS IN BODY SHAME

A cartoon taped up in my study shows a baby sitting in front of a full-length mirror, thinking: "This diaper makes my butt look big." The caption on top of the picture says, "It begins."

Shaming messages about the body don't start quite that early, but females are especially hard hit by messages that we're not okay looking the way we do. The pressures to look a certain way are everywhere, and we internalize the shaming messages of others until the enemy has outposts in our own heads. Let's look closely at the subject of appearance—how we feel about our "looks" and being looked at.

### God Made the Elephant Gray

When my friend Mary was in junior high school, her home economics teacher instructed the all-female class about buying fabric for a dress they would be making in class. "When you go to the fabric store, girls, keep this in mind," she said. "God made the canary yellow and He made the elephant gray!"

God's wisdom in the animal world, the teacher went on to explain, meant that regular-sized girls should choose fabrics in the

bright colors of our feathered friends. But large girls should remember that God made the elephant gray—and should choose
solid, dark colors accordingly.

In one fell swoop, the teacher compared the larger girls to ele-
phants (and, by association, to other lumbering gray animals like the
hippo and rhinoceros), and instructed them to not draw attention
to themselves. Hers was a prescription to hide out in drabness, a lesson in shame. My friend tells me that her teacher's words still come
back to her when she shops for clothes.

## Boney Maroney

Skinny girls are not immune to shaming messages. Despite my vo-
racious eating habits, I was unable to gain weight growing up. I was
"underdeveloped," and my peers taunted me with the lyrics of a
popular song of the day:

> *I got a girl name of Boney Maroney*
> *She's as skinny as a stick of macaroni!*

More painful to me were adult insensitivities. When I was a non-
budding adolescent, an uncle walked in on me while I was changing into a bathing suit in the bedroom of his apartment. I was stark
naked. I folded my arms in front of the breasts I didn't have and
yelled, "Get out!" I'm sure I sounded rude, but I was upset. My
uncle stood solidly in place, looked directly at me, and said coolly,
"Don't worry, Harriet. You have nothing to see."

In our fat-loathing culture where women die to be thin, it's
hard to imagine skinny girls being on the receiving end of shaming
messages. But it's not uncommon, even in adulthood. I hear from
many women who are significantly underweight, eat well, and can't
gain another pound. A skinny woman may feel very self-conscious

about her appearance because people sometimes assume she has an eating disorder or that she's a diet freak. When she's in the gym or locker room, she may hear frequent comments like "You're skin and bones!" or "I'll bet you weigh less than my German shepherd!"

These remarks are felt as shaming even though they are well-intentioned. Many people think that being thin is ideal and assume that—as with money—you can't have too much of a good thing. But any large departure from the norm, any difference that makes a difference, can become a target for shame. I'm reminded of a man I saw in therapy who towers over other men. He is constantly on the receiving end of quips such as "What's the weather like up there?" Or "Haven't you grown since I last saw you?" No one seems to consider that he might find both his height and their remarks painful—but he does. Most people would undoubtedly restrain their urge to comment if he was unusually short.

## "Get Out and Walk, Fat-Ass!"

If we are overweight, we're especially likely to be on the receiving end of shaming or taunting messages. Such messages hit hardest during childhood and adolescence. Most young people are dreadfully insecure themselves and always on the lookout for someone to dump their anxiety on, usually in the form of shaming.

But adults, too, are anxious and insecure, and shaming comments don't stop just because you're out of school and have your own apartment. "Fat people today are still on the receiving end of vitriol once reserved for seventeenth-century witches," author Natalie Kusz tells us from firsthand experience. Once, while she was idling her car at a traffic light, a driver alongside her shouted, "Get out and walk, fat-ass!" She's repeatedly had grocery cashiers hold up her purchases and loudly say, "I guess you didn't notice the low-calorie version."

Kusz writes with forceful candor about her decision to abandon the weight-loss life. She is no Pollyanna on the risks of obesity, but she's clear about what the unsuccessful fight against fat has cost her, and where she now stands. (Her motto: "They don't put your weight on your tombstone.") I was especially interested to learn that for Kusz, the most shaming of all admonitions is the well-intentioned disapproval of a friend—the one who leans a narrow hand on your arm and murmurs, "I hope this doesn't hurt your feelings, but I love you and I'm concerned about your weight." One can flee the stranger who yells "fat-ass" and never see him again, Kusz observes. But with friends we feel safe and relaxed, and therefore more vulnerable to feeling betrayed.

"*Why?*" is the question that Kusz finds unfathomable. Not why people say what they do—but why they think their efforts might be effective. She writes:

> Is it likely that in 38 years of living I have never once noticed my own corpulence? Or that I have somehow missed those alarmist hourly news reports on obesity ("Americans are fatter than ever!"), weight-loss studies, and the mortal (and, some believe, moral) risks of overweight? Perhaps they think I am having so much fun living the fat life (what with all those swanky clothes, adoring fans and male model escorts) that I've neglected subtle details such as creaky knees and a pendulous, unfashionable belly. Last possibility: that to weigh in (so to speak) on a fat person's self-style is compulsory, a form of intervention similar to that imposed on alcoholics, drug addicts, gamblers—on anyone, in short, without the strength of will to make good choices on her own.

Kusz notes that doctors have an especially difficult time restraining themselves from repeated lectures on the health risks of obesity.

"Doctors admonish me at every visit," she writes, "until I mention the fat ladies I know who, afraid of being shamed, never brave a medical office until they are too sick to be helped much at all."

Shame, even more than fear, keeps people from showing up. Of course, a doctor is responsible for putting forth the facts about risky and unhealthy behavior. But that is different from admonishing, lecturing, or hammering in the point after it has already clearly been made. My work with women confirms Kusz's observations. The fear of being shamed by a doctor is greater than the fear of avoiding the doctor—and thereby risking disability or death.


## MCDONALD'S VS. SUBWAY: SHEILA'S STORY

Sheila initially sought my help for work-related problems that had nothing to do with her weight. She was, in her words, a "super-sized chick" who in her thirties wanted affirmation for her ample presence in a diet-crazed world. There was a lot she liked about her size. She was physically strong and felt a kind of power in her large presence. She liked defying stereotypes, taking up space in the world, and setting an example of pride. She had attracted several boyfriends because of her size.

There were also things that Sheila didn't like about her weight. She hated how out of breath she became when she walked up stairs. Nor did she feel good about terrible eating habits that she felt helpless to change. "I'm a fast-food addict," she told me. "I live off McDonald's hamburgers, shakes, and fries." She mentioned that there was a Subway down the street from her workplace, a healthier option among the fast-food chains. "I'd love to get a grilled chicken sandwich there," she told me, "but they don't have a drive-through window, so Subway is out." She explained that she was too self-conscious to get out of her car, walk inside, order a sandwich, and walk back to the car.

Sheila presented quite a paradox. Here was a woman who could steal the show on the dance floor and light up a room with her enormous vitality and strong presence. She dressed with a dramatic flair that called attention to herself. She was comfortable being looked at in situations where others might feel self-conscious, such as public speaking or fund-raising. But Sheila had this one area of acute self-consciousness and vulnerability. She wouldn't go to Subway or any other fast-food chain that lacked a drive-through because in this particular context, she couldn't tolerate being watched. "I tried to go to Subway a few times when I was really in the mood for one of their sandwiches," she told me, "but I sat in the car paralyzed with anxiety. Then I drove to McDonald's for a Quarter Pounder with cheese." This was before McDonald's offered anything in the way of healthy choices.

Sheila was aware of the shame that fueled her anxiety. Even a drive-through, which eliminated the fear factor, didn't entirely protect her from this shame. When she would pick up her double order of burgers and fries at the drive-through at McDonald's, she would sometimes toss off a comment like "This is for my kids." Sheila knew that the person behind the window couldn't care less who was going to eat the food. Yet she felt compelled to suggest that the food wasn't for her.

## Dieting for Dollars

Ever since she had begun to gain weight in high school, Sheila's parents had been focused on her size and appearance. She told me that she couldn't begin to count the number of times they told her what a beauty she'd be if she'd only slim down because she had "such a pretty face." Shortly after Sheila started therapy with me, her parents had offered to pay her one hundred dollars for every five pounds she lost. "Mom and I are both worried about your health," her father had told her. "We'd like to offer this incentive." He suggested that they keep a chart by the scale in their bathroom so that when Sheila visited them, they could keep a record of pounds lost and money earned.

As Kusz reminds us, shaming often comes packaged as help. Sheila's first response was to go numb. "That's tempting," she said to her father," without registering any particular emotional response. "I'll think about it."

The offer was indeed tempting. Sheila had no savings, and she worried constantly about money. But the longer she sat with her father's words, the worse she felt. When I saw her in therapy later that week, she was in touch with how demeaned and shamed the offer made her feel. Her parents' involvement with her body and weight loss had always seemed excessive to her. Now Sheila felt a boundary had been crossed that left her feeling as if she didn't want to visit her parents for a long time.

## Accumulated Shame

"Whose body is it?" Sheila asked at her next therapy session. "I feel like my parents don't respect my boundaries. They're in my space. The idea of a chart in the bathroom makes me ill."

One association led to another. There had been significant boundary violations in Sheila's past, many associated with the body. "My father always refused to close the bathroom door when he urinated," she told me, "and he'd spank my bare bottom until I was twelve." The spankings humiliated her more than they hurt. They also made Sheila quite anxious, as she had a strong feeling that these spankings were erotically tinged for her father. He also made sexual comments both about her developing body and her friends' breasts. Not once did her mother stand up to him about these or other inappropriate, shaming behaviors.

Shame about how we look—and/or anxiety about being looked at—is most deeply felt when we have suffered previous humiliations or violations of the body, remembered or not. The offer to pay Sheila for losing weight, shaming in itself, landed on top of the accumulated vulnerability from these earlier violations. Shame is the fastest route back to childhood, to earlier incidents where we were speechless with shame and rage, and powerless to protest.

## Taking a Stand

Sheila turned down her parents' offer. This act represented a huge move from shame to pride. She handled the situation with enormous courage. Initially she planned to send an e-mail saying, "Thanks, but no thanks," and then avoid her parents entirely for a while. Instead she prepared herself for a face-to-face conversation.

Sheila kept it simple—always a good way to start. She dropped by her parents' home after dinner one evening and said, "Mom and Dad, I've thought about your offer to pay me for losing weight. I know that you're both trying to be helpful. But I'm just not comfortable with it and I've decided to pass." When her dad asked why, she said simply and without apology, "It just doesn't feel right to me."

He demanded to know the "logic" of her decision. To her credit, Sheila avoided arguing or trying to make her case, since she knew from experience that such efforts would go nowhere. She said, "Dad, I don't really know how to explain it. I can only tell you that your offer doesn't feel right to me. It's just how I feel."

"You've *never* been able to take our help!" her mother said accusingly.

"Mom, I need to deal with my eating and my weight in my own way. If I want any advice or encouragement from you or Dad, I'll ask you for it." Sheila said this calmly, without anger or blame.

She had rehearsed what she would say in therapy, but still, her heart was beating so fast, she thought she might go into cardiac arrest.

Predictably, her parents reacted defensively. They accused Sheila of being ungrateful, unmotivated, and immature. "Sheila, you're just plain wrong," her mother proclaimed. "If you could manage this yourself, you would have lost weight a long time ago."

"We offer to help you," her dad added, "and you act like *we're* the bad guys. That's crazy!"

With great effort, Sheila resisted getting defensive in return. She avoided the usual reflexive pitfalls, such as trying to convince her parents of her viewpoint, getting angry, or withdrawing. She was well prepared to underreact rather than overreact to her parents' obnoxious statements, which simply reflected their high level of anxiety.

She said calmly, "My intention isn't to insult you and I know that you aren't trying to insult me. But crazy or not, your offer doesn't feel good to me."

"You're out to lunch!" her mother muttered, an interesting metaphor in Sheila's case. "Do what you want—you always do anyway." I imagine Sheila's mother was quite anxious about hearing Sheila speak up so assertively, when she herself had never been able to speak firmly to her husband and hold her own ground.

"You're so oversensitive!" were her father's final words. "Most people would be grateful for such a generous offer!"

"Well," said Sheila, "I hope you'll honor my request even if you don't agree with me. You can help me most by understanding that if I want help or advice from you about losing weight, I'll ask for it." Then she changed the subject to a neutral topic by asking her mother where she had purchased the blinds in the kitchen, because she was thinking of buying a similar kind for her apartment.

## One Thing Leads to Another

Speaking assertively inspired Sheila to speak even more bravely. Taking courage to the limits, she opened up another conversation with her father about the violations of her childhood. Confronting painful issues from the past can sometimes help us build pride where shame used to flourish. But the process requires us to face fear and walk through it.

Sheila started the conversation when her dad was flipping through the TV channels. Her father was a poor listener, but she recalled that he did a bit better when he didn't feel the pressure of eye-to-eye contact. The conversations that had gone well in the past had happened in the car, doing dishes, while the TV was on, or with some other distraction in place. So one night, in the TV room after dinner, Sheila jumped in.

"Dad," she began, "I was thinking about your comment the other day that I was oversensitive when I turned down your offer to pay me for losing weight. Maybe someone else would be grateful, like you said."

Sheila paused, took a couple of deep breaths, and then continued. "It got me wondering if maybe my extra sensitivity relates to some painful things that happened in our family in the past." Staring at the TV, her dad said, "I don't know what you're talking about."

"Dad, you didn't respect my boundaries when I was growing up," Sheila went on. "You left the door open when you urinated, even after I asked you to close it. You gave me those spankings that felt humiliating to me. And you made comments about my body and about my friends' breasts. These behaviors of yours left me with a lot of anxiety and anger. So perhaps I'm especially sensitive to wanting my boundaries respected when I say I would like you and Mom to back off about my weight and let me deal with it in my own way."

The entire time she spoke, Sheila's father channel-surfed as though his life depended on it. Now he turned sharply to look at her. "You have one amazing imagination," he spit out. Before she could respond, he rose from his armchair and stalked out of the room. As Sheila watched him go, she realized she was shaking.

Few actions evoke more anxiety than carefully opening a conversation about past harm. It is most difficult if one tries to be one's most mature self in the process. Angry, hit-and-run confrontations are easier, because they reflect and elicit pure reactivity. No one is holding on to the connection and truly inviting the other person to think and to stay in the conversation over time. If you shame the shamer or blame the blamer, you let him off the hook because there is no chance he will ever consider what you are saying.

As time went on, I offered Sheila support, suggestions, and perspective on the several conversations she opened with her parents. Sheila also learned more about other relatives who had struggled with "out-of-controlness" in some way—a big theme in Sheila's family. She took each conversation only so far and no further, since she was the best judge of how much anxiety and emotional intensity she could manage.

## Letting Go of Expectations

In choosing speech over silence, Sheila didn't get the response she wanted and hoped for from either parent. Getting the "right response" is rarely our reward for speaking when afraid. Sheila understood from the outset that her parents would most likely not be able to listen with an open heart, apologize, or even validate her reality. They were too ashamed themselves.

To avoid the experience of shame, wrongdoers will usually wrap themselves in layers of rationalization and denial. They will blame someone else, or even deny that the bad thing occurred at all.

Shame, in contrast to guilt, feels so intolerable that most people who have done serious harm won't "go there" and are thus unable to reflect on their contribution to hurting another family member. Most people can apologize for what they have done (guilt). Few can apologize for who they *are* (shame).

But what mattered was that Sheila spoke up. She spoke not because she expected "results" but because she needed to reclaim her own sense of honor, pride, and self-regard. Whenever we speak to an especially painful and loaded issue, we need to let go of any expectations of getting the apology or validation we want. Neither may be forthcoming, now or ever. We will come from a more solid place if we speak to preserve our own well-being and integrity. The sound of our own voice, speaking our own truth, is what we most need to hear.

## Back to Subway

Does it surprise you to learn that shortly after initiating these conversations with her parents, Sheila walked through the doors of Subway? During one therapy session, as she once again bemoaned her "McDonald's addiction," I decided to push her.

"The courage you've shown in talking to your parents is amazing," I told her. "You can get out of the car and walk into Subway. I promise you can do it."

"No, I can't!" she protested. "I'm too anxious and self-conscious. I'll just sit in the parking lot, paralyzed."

"How long do you think you'll stay paralyzed?" I asked her. "Ten minutes, an hour, the entire afternoon?"

It was a serious question. People can stay emotionally paralyzed for only so long. Anxiety will eventually subside. Plus, we weren't talking about a bona fide, bone-rattling phobia here. This was merely fear.

Sheila protested and I pushed. "So what if you feel scared, ashamed, and full of dread?" I said lightly. "Just do it. You'll live. Consider it an assignment. Then we'll talk about how it went."

My message was "Feel the fear, the shame, the paralysis, whatever, but get out of the car and buy the sandwich." I pushed her with humor, but I was also tough. It's not my ordinary therapeutic style to direct a client in this way, especially not a woman who already had a history of intrusiveness and violation. But my intuition told me to lean on her.

Sheila did it. She came back the next week and told me that it was the funniest thing, but when she pulled up to Subway, she felt no resistance at all to going inside and ordering herself a grilled chicken sandwich on a bun, with extra lettuce and tomato. "Amazing," she said. "It was nothing—it was like picking up my dry cleaning. I didn't feel any anxiety. I didn't think about people watching me. Nothing."

"So what did you learn from this?" I asked. Perhaps there was an important lesson here.

Sheila paused. She looked deep in thought. Finally she spoke.

"I learned that I don't even like their goddamn sandwiches," she said. And then, a few minutes later, "Maybe I should learn to cook."

## A Postscript

Are you wondering if Sheila lost weight? Yes, some. She cut out fast food and started eating more conscientiously. One step in a healthful direction (eating well) inspired another (exercising). She had also reflected quite a bit on the difficulties with self-regulation that plagued so many of her family members. She gained some satisfaction from making more thoughtful decisions about what she put in her mouth.

In finding a strong voice with her parents, and speaking directly to the sense of violation she had experienced as a child, Sheila felt on more solid ground as a person, and felt more committed to treating her own body lovingly and with care. Although her parents never apologized for their behaviors, they stopped bringing up her weight, and the relationship began to feel more adult-to-adult. While I haven't seen Sheila in many years, I trust she's still a super-sized chick, stealing the show on any dance floor with her grace and large appetite for life.

## WHAT'S THE REAL ISSUE HERE?

Sometimes we don't like our appearance simply because we've learned not to. Societal norms, transmitted through the family, get internalized and become part of us. The dominant culture defines what's beautiful (or at least acceptable) and what's not. If we're lucky, we will have a whole community of strong people challenging the definitions of the dominant group ("Black is beautiful!"). Shame is replaced by pride as new meanings of beauty get established.

Sometimes, though, our feelings about our appearance have little to do with anything about our physical selves at all. We're anxious, insecure, or upset about something else. Shame and self-loathing get focused on the body, but the true sources of anxiety are obscured from view. Anytime we become anxiously over-focused on this or that part of our body or appearance, it's a good bet that we are underfocused on something else, past or present, that we don't want to look at.

### Lori: How Much Do Looks Matter?

Consider Lori, who wrote me a lengthy letter while I was working as an advice columnist for *New Woman Magazine*. Lori described herself as "a dumpy twenty-seven-year-old woman with matronly breasts, a big behind, and a plain face." She avoided social situations and had been in therapy for years because she desperately wanted to marry but felt overwhelming anxiety about meeting men. Her shame about her appearance filled the pages, as did her worry about staying single. She wrote, "My therapist tells me that heavy, plain-looking women get married as frequently as gorgeous women do, but I know I'll never get married and it makes my whole life miserable. I can't come to terms with my bad luck."

Of course, I agreed with her therapist. Just spend an afternoon people-watching in a crowded shopping mall, and you'll see wedding rings on women of every size, shape, and form. Some men, it's true, won't look twice at a woman who isn't beautiful or sexy by conventional standards. And to some extent, marriage is a competitive venture. Most attractive women have a larger pool of men to choose from than do women who are considered plain. The same is true for younger women and high-income men. That said, love and marriage are about finding *one* person you hope will be your life partner. In this venture, physical appearance is less important than a wealth of other factors that shape our capacity to love and be loved. Lori's problem is her shame-driven perspective on herself.

How much *do* looks count? Appearance matters most in early encounters, but least in the enduring connections of friendship, love, and marriage. A woman's physical beauty—or lack of it—tells us virtually nothing about how her relationship will fare over time. In my thirty years of practice as a psychotherapist, I have not once seen a connection between a woman's conventional attractiveness and the intimacy, depth, resilience, passion, tenderness, or endurance of her intimate relationship.

## The Real Ingredients of Attractiveness

Appearance goes way beyond our immutable physical characteristics. Our attractiveness to others is powerfully influenced by our confidence, warmth, character, intelligence, personality, spirit, and style, as well as more elusive "vibes" that can't be named. How a woman feels about herself comes through. The fact that Lori feels so negatively about herself will certainly affect how others respond to her. But even more to the point, Lori's negative, self-deprecating perception of how she looks isn't good for *her*.

Lori needs to do the best with what she has and move on. It's not easy for her to accept and love herself when she feels so bad about her appearance, but by staying overfocused on her appearance, she'll stay *underfocused* on other important issues. When anxiety and shame land with a big thud on any one issue, we can be sure we are ignoring others.

I responded to Lori with some hard questions: What talents and abilities does she want to develop over the next few years? What are her work and career goals? What are her values and beliefs about being a good sister, daughter, aunt, or cousin? What connections does she have in her neighborhood and community? What is the importance of friendship in her life? Does she take good care of herself? What sort of home does she want to create for herself? Is she living healthfully? What brings her pleasure or joy? Is she being useful to others—perhaps the greatest of all antidotes to the pain of self-absorption.

If Lori stays attached to the false belief that her looks are the problem—and that marriage is the solution—she may spend more years in therapy blaming her appearance for her unhappiness. The fact is, many gorgeous, married women are also lonely and miserable. Many plain, single women are joyful and richly connected. If Lori has a good heart, and if she moves forward in her life, she will find other people of a similar nature—whether she marries or not.

## LIFE LESSONS FROM SUMMER CAMP

The body—and how it appears in the eyes of the self and others—was put into perspective for me one summer in my late teens. I worked as a counselor at a camp called Wagon Road in upstate New York. This opportunity provided me experiences that I've never forgotten. Not that I was out to learn anything. In fact, I ended up at Wagon Road entirely by chance. Another summer job had fallen through at the last minute, and my father, who worked at the New York State Employment Agency, got me this job. I was clueless as to what he had signed me up for.

Wagon Road, as it turned out, was for kids with serious illnesses and disabilities of every kind. Some of the children had diagnoses that were familiar to me: muscular dystrophy, cerebral palsy, or "deaf, dumb, and blind." Others had illnesses or disorders with names I'd never heard of. Many had missing limbs and major deformities, along with severe emotional limitations. Everyone had *something* that precluded participation in mainstream summer programs.

The counselors arrived at the campgrounds several days earlier than the campers to settle in and get oriented. I was assigned to the job of co-counselor of one of the girls' cabins. Finally, the first day of camp arrived, and a big bus from Port Authority in New York lumbered in to the campgrounds. One by one, the kids were unloaded. Nothing I was told or had imagined prepared me for the visceral shock of watching these children emerge into the sunlight. "Oh my God" were the words I said to myself over and over as I steeled myself for the eight weeks ahead. What had I gotten myself into? "Oh my God."

The first camper I wheeled into my cabin was named Stephanie. She had multiple facial anomalies and stumps for arms and legs. Her birth parents did not take her home from the hospital where she was born, and she was not adoptable. She was being raised in an institution. Yet it was immediately obvious that she was one of these remarkably resilient kids who had developed enormous spunk and personality. In fact, I noticed that all the kids looked happy to be there.

Was it a day—or less than an hour—before my initial reaction of shock and fear seemed like a dim memory? How quickly this world became as normal as any other! Every child looked so different that no child looked different at all. The only difference that seemed to matter was that some of the kids needed a lot more help than others, or required special equipment to lift them from the bed to the wheelchair.

Every kid looked fine to me, and apparently they looked just fine to one another. I didn't see the usual formation of cliques, of insiders or outsiders. There were no indications of shame, self-pity, or pity for others. The children woke up each morning eager to connect and participate in activities.

These kids seemed not to judge one another. They had, as you might imagine, a huge tolerance for differences. The following summer I worked in a camp with "regular" kids and watched girls of the same age make themselves miserable for some failure they felt regarding their size or skin or hair, or lack of athleticism in some activity like swimming or volleyball. These girls were in a "normal" context in which they exaggerated amazingly minor differences. And from these minor differences sprouted hierarchies and status, insiders and outsiders, the popular and unpopular—the full range of social anxiety and misery.

## The Right to Be Different

The right to be different, whether by choice or necessity, is our greatest right as human beings. And dealing with differences is the greatest of all human challenges. People react anxiously and fearfully to differences. We learn to hate, glorify, deny, exaggerate, or eradicate a difference. Or we try to get comfortable by shaming the different person or group. Wagon Road was a context where even the most dramatic difference was "just a difference." By working there, I learned that such a context really could exist—and how much context mattered.

I also observed some inspiring and amazing examples of kids resisting shame. I visited Stephanie after camp was over and recall a particular fall afternoon when I was pushing her in her wheelchair along the grounds of Bellevue Hospital. A "rich lady" (she looked like a caricature) passed us on the path, stooped down to eye level with Stephanie, and pinched her cheek. "Why, aren't you cute, my dear," she said with that false brightness that people sometimes use with the very old and the very young. "Aren't you *cute!*"

I was stunned. How could she say such a thing to Stephanie? Why did she feel the need to say anything at all? Probably this woman caught herself staring, became anxious, and felt she had to say something. It also bothered me that she would pinch the cheek of a child who couldn't pinch back. I found the whole incident to be enormously shaming.

But there was no uncomfortable silence, no time for me to wonder how to respond, or whether I should say anything at all. For Stephanie, who was all of nine at the time, looked the woman in the eye and spoke up. "Why are you saying that to me, lady?" she asked. "You know I'm not cute."

There was not one false note in Stephanie's response, which was totally free of anger, bitterness, or a wish to hurt back. It was merely an illustration of Stephanie's straight-shooting, no-holds-barred personality. She was simply "out there." As we proceeded down the path, Stephanie said matter-of-factly, "When people look at me they don't know what to say, so they say really stupid things." She understood what many adults don't—that when people say shaming, insensitive things, it's nothing personal. It's about them, not you.

Our society doesn't promote self-acceptance and it never will. First of all, self-acceptance doesn't sell products. Capitalism would fall if we liked ourselves the way we are now. Also, people who feel shamed and inadequate themselves tend to pass it on. I'm sure you've noticed that many individuals and groups try to enhance their self-esteem by diminishing others.

Sometimes, midlife loosens body shame and refocuses our energy. As one fifty-six-year-old teacher puts it, "I know I'd feel better if I could lose fifteen pounds. But at the same time, I'm old enough to know it's all such bullshit." If nothing else, middle age will bring you far more serious things to worry about than your feta cheese thighs. But some women feel even more body shame as they age, so don't sit passively around and wait for the years to bring you greater wisdom and perspective. Many folks do get past appearance and body hang-ups, but it requires the will to keep swimming upstream against a strong cultural tide.

## SPEAKING THE UNSPEAKABLE

I can't conclude a chapter on body shame without posing this question:

What part of the female body is the location of so much anxiety and shame that it is virtually unspeakable? Take a guess.

Nope, not the vagina.

It's the vulva.

What, you say?

Yes, the vulva, the external female genitalia that includes the mons, the labia, the clitoris, and the perineum. The vulva is standard female equipment. So why can't we admit it?

## The Whatchamacallit Problem

"My husband doesn't like my vagina," Louise tells me, eyes down. "He says it's messy and complicated. It's like he needs a road map to find his way around. And I hate feeling like a traffic cop. I feel like there's something wrong or different about me that he can't find his way around."

I try to picture a messy and complicated vagina, but to no avail. My client is a professor and a scholar. She knows her vagina from her vulva. She is too uncomfortable to use the correct word, so I invite her to do so, by asking simply, "A complicated *vagina?*"

She turns red and says, almost angrily, "I'm talking about—you know—*that outside stuff.*"

"You mean your vulva?" I ask.

"Yes, yes, of course," she says.

*That outside stuff?* Why such confused, undifferentiated, self-deprecating language for the vulva? Like most of us, Louise was raised on some variation of "boys have a penis and girls have a vagina." To quote from a popular book of the day: "A girl has two ovaries, a uterus, and a vagina which are her sex organs. A boy's sex organs are a penis and testicles. One of the first changes (at puberty) will be *the growth of hair around the vaginal opening of the girl*" (italics mine). Such partial and inaccurate labeling of female genitalia might inspire any pubescent girl to sit on the bathroom floor with a mirror and conclude that she is a freak. Louise had had just such a terrible experience herself.

Over the long course of therapy, Louise and I had had many conversations about anatomy and sexuality. When she was little, she had looked at her brother's penis with some envy because it was so neat and simple. "It was easy to figure out. No confusing and hidden parts. It was all on the outside and open to inspection." When I made the point that what she had "on the outside" was also open to inspection, but was never named, she responded with immediate recognition. "Yes, everyone knows that men have a penis and everyone can say the word. But the only word that people will say to describe what women have is 'vagina.' "

"You, too?" I asked.

"Me, too," she replied.

The shame and anxious confusion Louise felt about her vulva persisted into adulthood. She wouldn't get undressed in a locker room if other women were present. She hated the fact that her inner labia "peeked out like a turkey wattle." Of course, heterosexual women almost never have the opportunity to get accurate visual information (that is, from comparison with other women) that allows us to appreciate our anatomical variability. As to the "what's normal?" question, vulvas differ widely in style, color, size, and proportion, and many include "turkey wattles."

A sexual trauma also fueled Louise's shameful feeling of being different. When she was in middle school, her father came into her room at night over a period of several days when her mother was away caring for her own dying mother. During this time her father tickled her legs and her vulva "to help her relax." She was in therapy at the time and had tried to circle around her own traumatic incident by mentioning that she had a friend whose dad may have touched her between her legs. "Are you trying to say that her dad touched her vagina?" the therapist asked. Louise clutched and said her friend was probably making it up. She changed the subject.

Louise went home and looked up the word "vagina" in the dictionary. She felt dizzy with shame and confusion. Her father hadn't touched her *there*. Was she making a big deal out of nothing? She knew the word "labia," which had been defined for her as "the lips that protect the vagina." So did this mean that her dad had merely touched the place protecting the place he shouldn't touch? Her reality, first shaken by the sexual violation, was further mystified by the absence of a shared and comfortable vocabulary to facilitate clear thinking and clear conversation. She basically shut down with this therapist, and didn't speak of the traumatic incident until her work with me.

When we feel prohibited from speaking clearly, we also can't think clearly. Having accurate language to distinguish the vulva from the vagina is crucial for *every* girl, even when there has been no history of boundary violations. The persistent misuse of the word "vagina" impairs a girl's capacity to develop an accurate and differentiated "map" of her internal and external genitals. The fact that a girl's own exploration of her genitals is not corroborated by information from her environment also creates body shame and anxiety about sexuality. When a confusing sexual violation does occur ("Why is this happening to me? How can I make sense of it? Why is it a secret?"), the false and inaccurate labeling of female genitals increases shame and complicates healing.

## Raising Vulva Consciousness

Vulva—what's that? When my friend Nancy was diagnosed with vestibular adenitis, an uncommon disease of the unspeakable parts, she called the National Institutes of Health to gather more information. She presented the facts to the woman in charge of directing her call. "Vulva?" the woman repeated querulously. "Vulva? Is that heart and lungs?"

My first serious attempt to raise vulva consciousness was directed toward my professional colleagues. After joining the staff of the Menninger Clinic, I published a paper called "Parental Misla-beling of Female Genitals as a Determinant of Penis Envy and Learning Inhibitions in Women." I illustrated how the failure to ac-curately label a girl's external genitalia contributes to shame and confusion about sexuality, as well as to inhibitions about looking and learning. The article appeared in 1974 in a prestigious psycho-analytic journal and was met with a dignified fraternal silence.

I was undaunted. I have continued over the decades to encour-age parents to say vagina when they mean *that* and vulva when they mean *that*. Some educated adults still report never having heard the word "vulva," including a large number who think the term refers to a Swedish automobile. Even more interesting are the majority of folks who *do* know the word but are too uncomfortable to use it.

When I ask parents why they don't tell their daughters that they have a vulva which includes the clitoris, I hear an imaginative array of excuses, the most common being, "I don't like the word." Here are some others:

Telling my daughter about her vulva and clitoris is like telling her to go masturbate.

Vulva is a medical term. It's sort of technical. I don't want to burden her with words that her friends don't know. (This one from parents who taught their small daughter about ovaries and Fallopian tubes.)

The vagina is her sex organ. It's related to intercourse and re-production. That's all she needs to know about.

If I use the term "vulva," she'll spread the news to her class-mates and how will we deal with that? And I can't tell her about something that tiny [her clitoris]. I'm not even sure how to pronounce it.

In Freud's time, the only word in *Webster's Dictionary* to refer to female genitals was "vagina." The words "vulva," "clitoris," and "labia" were nowhere to be found. One might question how pride in female sexuality could flourish at a time when our language did not include words for the parts of the female anatomy most richly endowed with sensory nerve endings and with no function but that of sensual pleasure.

Although the appropriate additions to *Webster's* have since been made, little has changed, linguistically speaking, since Freud's day. It is true that Americans do not surgically remove the clitoris and labia, as is the case with millions of girls and women in other cultures. Instead we do the job linguistically—a psychological genital mutilation, if you will. Language can be as powerful and swift as the surgeon's knife. What is not named does not exist.

## The Vagina Monologues?

I've been doggedly raising vulva consciousness since the late 1960s, publishing and lecturing on the importance of accurate labeling of the vulva, which includes the labia and clitoris. I had reason to believe I was making progress. But when I saw *The Vagina Monologues* with my husband in New York City, I felt I had fallen down the rabbit hole of Alice in Wonderland. Here was a play whose purpose was purportedly to restore pride in female genitals—including pride in naming—and it could not have been more obfuscating of genital reality.

Playwright Eve Ensler has made enormous contributions to women. It's not Ensler but rather her audience I want to focus on, the tens of thousands of women and men who watched the play, or listened to the conversation surrounding it, and pretended that nothing was amiss—or worse, didn't *know* that anything was amiss. As my friend Emily Kofron wrote in an unpublished letter to *Ms.* magazine:

Is there a sudden mass feminist amnesia about the difference between a vagina and a vulva? I doubt that men would tolerate a supposed celebration of their sexuality that confused a scrotum or testicle with a penis. Are we women so accustomed to subordination that we remain pathetically grateful for any acknowledgment of our female genitalia, no matter how inaccurate?

Some people watching the play did *not* suffer from genital amnesia in the naming department. A woman named Shelley True may have said it best in an online article published on www.thingsihate.com. True had taken her seventeen year old daughter to the play in a theater packed with a diverse audience gathered together in the pursuit of genital anecdotes. She listened to the opening questions that Eve Ensler asked women. "What would your vagina wear?" "What would your vagina say?"

"What? Okay," True thought, "so these questions were icebreakers to get women to talk about their vaginas." But when the stories started, especially the one about a husband insisting a woman shave her vagina, True was horrified. "Shave a vagina? What are you shaving off a vagina? Wouldn't you need some kind of specialty razor, maybe a larger version of those mail order nose hair trimmers? My God!"

While some of the stories were about the vagina, it didn't take long for True to realize that you had to substitute the word "vulva" for "vagina" for most of the play to make any sense at all.

I wanted to stand on my chair and announce, "Listen to me, it's vulva, not vagina. You're talking about vulvas!" I wanted to lead a chant of "Vul-va, vul-va!" But I figured my 17-year-old would slink out and never speak to me again. I kept thinking I must be mishearing these people. When the performance was over my daughter turned to me and said, "Vulva."

Then there were T-shirts, buttons, and "chocolate vaginas" for sale. True purchased the chocolate to bring home to her husband. Without prompting, he immediately identified the candy as a vulva. "A dark day for female twat scholarship," True writes. "He doesn't even *have* one!"

## The Fear of Female Sexuality

How can this little two-syllable word be surrounded by such fear and confusion? After all, it's more euphonic and easier to say than the three-syllable vagina. Freud himself recognized the anxiety that the vulva seemed to inspire and recalled a passage from Rabelais in which the exhibition of a woman's vulva put the devil himself in flight. Psychoanalytic theorists believe that male castration anxiety is one source of the fear, noting it's the "hairy maternal vulva," and not the vagina (which is invisible to inspection) that may give the impression of a "wound" and may arouse the little boy's fear that his penis may be lost.

Freud's theories aside, I would posit that the vulva is so threatening because it is the primary source of female sexual pleasure, the girl's first site of masturbation and sexual self-discovery, separate from intercourse or reproduction. Many parents are quite anxious about acknowledging that their young daughter is a sexual individual who has curiosity about and pleasure with her genitals, and the dread and denial of female sexuality has been well documented by scholars in various disciplines. In any case, we don't need to agree on why we fear something in order to make a positive change.

## Would You Like to Join the V-Club? (V Is for Vulva)

I was in the locker room in the YWCA in Topeka, Kansas, when I overheard the following conversation:

"That's his *penis,* isn't it, Mommy?" squealed a preschool girl, pointing at a naked baby boy nearby. Her mother, more amused than embarrassed by her daughter's unabashed curiosity, answered in the affirmative.

"And what's *that?*" the girl asked, pointing now at the crotch of a naked little girl standing nearby.

"That's her vagina," her mother answered brightly, not missing a beat.

I cleared my throat to speak. I wanted to lean over to that mother and say, "Vagina! You must be kidding! Do you have X-ray vision, lady?" But I bit my tongue. I have a bad habit of correcting people's language, but I do try to restrain myself from lecturing strangers on their word choices in public places.

Instead, I started the V-Club decades ago with some wonderful women associated with the Women's Therapy Center in New York City. As president of the club, I invite all of you to become members. The criterion for membership is to use the words "vulva" and "vagina" correctly, and to encourage others to do the same. Sorry, there are no membership cards, T-shirts, or buttons. I can promise you, however, that if we ever do sell chocolates, a chocolate vulva will look like a vulva and a chocolate vagina will look like— hmmm—perhaps something like a tube of macaroni.

If you meet the criterion for membership, you'll have another hole punched in your Feminist Heaven card. You'll be a shame-buster, giving more power to women—which is also a gift to men. So here's the question, going back to the little girl in the locker room. What if you were standing there with the little girl who asked her mother, "And what's that?"

How would you answer her? Remember, to be larger than fear and shame we need to choose language, clarity, and self-definition over silence and mystification.

It's her *vulva*. We can say it out loud. We owe it to ourselves, and to girls and women of all ages, to use the right word.

# CHAPTER 10

# When Things Fall Apart:

## Facing Illness and Suffering

Your worst fears may never be realized. Or your worst worries may be realized and yet not be as terrible as you expected. You think you can't survive the breakup but you do. Your daughter has surgery and things are fine. Your son comes home at three in the morning—but he comes home. You make it through the thunderstorm and find your way back to town. The cancer was encapsulated; the doctors report they "got it all." Sometimes the light at the end of the tunnel really is a light, and not another approaching train.

But sooner or later the universe will send you a crash course in vulnerability, meaning that you—or someone you love—will get a great big lesson in fear and grief. Then you live with fear as a constant companion, or you have a close relationship with someone who does. You may face impending death, your own or someone else's. While such experiences are inevitably frightening and painful, there are things we can each do to live our life to the best of our possibilities.

## THE FEAR OF DEATH

Death is what many people fear the most. While Americans are said to rank the fear of public speaking higher than the fear of death, I'm quite certain this finding doesn't reflect the real truth. Folks who fill out surveys probably worry that they may soon be called upon to speak in public, but see no imminent danger of dying. As a test, just dangle them from the rooftop of a tall building and offer them the choice of falling head first to the pavement below or signing on for a public speaking engagement.

"I don't fear death itself," many people tell me, "just dying." Of course, people *do* fear death, because death ends a life—a monumental fact—and is therefore different from other anxiety-provoking events. Ian Frazier, in a humorous *New Yorker* article, describes death as "a no-win experience," noting that, "at the end of medical humiliations, physical suffering, money concerns, fear, and tedium of dying, one has no outcome to look forward to except being dead." Death, at least on this earthly plane, doesn't hold out the possibility of a better outcome in the future, as might another anxious event, such as divorce or unemployment.

Impending death may not seem all that scary if it comes as a gentle docking after a long life well lived. But who asks us? Death comes any time it pleases and is always a looming threat. Suffering is hardest when accompanied by such questions as "Why me?" "What did I do to deserve this?" and "How can life be so unfair to let me die so young (or in this way)?" Life isn't fair and neither is death. But if we let ourselves be consumed with questions of "fairness," we run the risk of digging ourselves deeper into despair, rather than discovering the opportunities for pleasure and meaning that are still available to us.

# THE MUSTARD SEED STORY

When Anne Morrow Lindbergh's infant son was kidnapped and murdered, only the story of the mustard seed helped her. A woman who has lost her baby asks a holy man if there is a cure for her grief. "Yes," he replies. "You must find a house that has never known sorrow, take a mustard seed from that house, and then you will be cured." The woman spent the rest of her life looking, but could never find a house that had not known sorrow.

I was young when I first heard this story and it made no sense to me. Suffering is not democratic. If you *were* to go house-to-house observing sorrow, you would not necessarily conclude that, oh, gee, you didn't have it so bad after all. On my block, for example, there is no house where a mother lost her infant to kidnapping and murder, nothing so terrible as that.

Today I understand that the mustard seed story is not about comparing your fate to the fate of others. Cycles of comparisons require attention to *differences*—like comparing your child's SAT scores to those of her classmates. The mustard seed story invites us to appreciate the *commonality* of suffering in the human family. It tells us that suffering defines the human condition, that when we sign on to living there is no possibility of escaping fear and grief. Indeed, the "cure" for fear and grief comes only in recognizing that there is no cure. You may consider your suffering "exceptional," but it is always part of the greater human condition.

Since Anne Morrow Lindbergh said that the parable of the mustard seed was all that helped her, I imagine the story allowed her to understand that the burden of grief is carried by the entire human family, that fear and suffering define the human condition as much as, if not more than, happiness and joy. In our most difficult moments, sometimes the most empowering thing we can do is to recognize our common powerlessness.

We all die someday. Despite our culture's emphasis on "control and mastery" we don't choose when we die or how—lightning, a tiger attack, a car accident, violence, disease, the natural failures of the body, or simply being in the wrong place at the wrong time. By letting go of our desire to control the course of the universe, we get back a sense of our place in it. Control is an illusion—a fact you will learn very fast if you become ill, or have things fall apart in some other way. When we understand vulnerability and suffering as an essential part of being human, our individual fate can be easier to manage.

## THE FALSE PATH OF COMPARISONS

Since most of us are not highly evolved spiritual beings, we tend to go house-to-house looking for someone who "has it worse" so we can feel better. Rather than appreciating human commonality, we will look for differences. You only have to turn on the television or read the newspaper to remind yourself that life has dealt other people a worse hand than your own.

Thumbing through my sixth grade diary, the record of a thoroughly miserable year, I found this quote I had typed and pasted on the page. "I used to cry because I had no shoes until I met a man who had no feet." Obviously, this gave me some comfort. But comparing our suffering to that of others offers temporary relief at best. Maybe it helped me on some days to think about footless people, but on other days I'd think about the girls in my class who had all their body parts plus boyfriends, and I'd feel worse.

That's how it works when your mind gets wrapped around comparisons. You are terrified about your son's future and ashamed that he's back on parole, so you get some relief when you meet a mother whose kid is in deeper trouble than yours. But tomorrow you will meet a mother who introduces you to her three beautiful daughters, beaming with good health—Sarah, the Guggenheim scholar; Anna, the neurosurgeon on the faculty of Harvard Medical School; and Julie, the astrophysicist who is fluent in Spanish, Bengali, and Russian and has just finished her second novel while on maternity leave from her prestigious job at NASA.

Of course, that family's good luck can change on a dime. They could be killed together in a van on the way to their splendid summer home on Cape Cod. The unpredictability of life may also reassure you, as may the fact that many people who "look good," and have all the outer trappings of happiness, are far more miserable than people who have "nothing." We don't have access to the emotional experience of those folks we are convinced have perfect lives. But ultimately the reassurances that come from any type of comparative ranking will offer you only the same temporary comfort as eating a hot fudge sundae or an entire box of Kraft macaroni and cheese.

When you're tempted to make comparisons, you should also remind yourself that if you get consumed by them, you may also fail to honor your own fear and suffering because you consider it minor. "I feel guilty being here," many therapy clients tell me, "when other people have much worse problems than mine." Or "Why have I fallen apart just because my relationship ended, when people are being blown up in Iraq? What's wrong with me?" Or, alternatively, comparisons may leave you unable to see personal grief as part of the collective experience of human suffering, because you're attached to the cry, "I've suffered more!"

Of course, individuals do suffer more or less, and differences need to be acknowledged. But hanging on to comparisons as a way to lift yourself out of fear and grief is the opposite of what the mustard seed story intends and what we can aim for.

## Is Suffering Shameful?

Last but not least, comparisons breed shame. Shame can overwhelm you if you measure yourself by the narrow cultural images that surround you, especially in the media. You're not healthy, beautiful, thin, rich, or productive enough. There's something wrong with you for not being more emotionally or physically "fit." You are essentially flawed because you have too much bad stuff happening to you, and you're not "getting over it" in the prescribed amount of time or the way other people seem to.

Shame can also make you feel obligated to deny your fear and grief, to tuck it away rather than give voice to it. As bell hooks notes, we may especially feel shame about grief that lingers: "Like a stain on our clothes, it marks us as flawed, imperfect. To cling to grief, to desire its expression, is to be out of sync with modern life, where the hip do not get bogged down in mourning."

And God forbid you should become "dependent," that is, more dependent than you think you should be, compared to others. As writer and disability activist Anne Finger points out, we learn that some dependencies are okay (a car, a hairdresser) and some are not (a wheelchair, an attendant to wash your hands and face). If you get mired in judgments, you may feel it's shameful at *your* age to need a cane, a nap, a pill, time off work, or a hearing aid. You may be ashamed for the simple fact that you need help.

In reality, every human being is dependent on the help and support of others. There's nothing shameful about recognizing how much we need each other—a fact we can deny when we're healthy and things are going along well. What's shameful is the myth that with the right "can-do" attitude, we can bootstrap our way to health, wealth, and happiness. Or that staying strong, vigorous, and youthful is what matters most, rather than cultivating acceptance for what is. Or that fear and suffering is weak, and that our job is to "take control of our lives" and "run the show." Surrender is not the American Way. We are expected to turn even the most terrifying experiences and unfathomable losses into an opportunity for personal growth. Writer Michael Ventura calls this our "consumer attitude" toward experience and notes that other cultures would find it unnatural.

We suffer more when we fail to appreciate that change, impermanence, loss, and death are all we can count on for sure. From any larger perspective, be it evolutionary, religious, or spiritual, we are all here for a very short time, less than an eye blink in the broad scheme of things, whether we die at age one or one hundred.

We have nobody's life to live but our own, so we all need to manage what fate hands us as well as we can—even when things fall apart, which they will. Few of us are evolved enough to live fully, mindfully, and peacefully in the face of crisis. But we can minimize the energy we spend comparing ourselves to others or feeling ashamed of our vulnerability, and maximize the energy we spend living as full and fulfilling a life as possible. It isn't easy. But there are ways of living honorably and meaningfully even when we're facing death.

## RHODA: LIVING WITH CHRONIC ILLNESS

Rhoda was in her early thirties when she came to see me in therapy. Three years earlier she had been diagnosed with a degenerative, chronic illness that, short of a future cure, would ultimately leave her totally debilitated and unable to care for herself. At the time of her diagnosis, she felt as if her life were over. Fear and depression flooded her. How could this happen? Everything she had taken for granted was turned totally upside down—her work, her daily habits, her finances, her sex life, her appearance, her independence, her notion of a bright and boundless future.

Rhoda had two best friends, Barbara and Evelyn. Together they had formed a loyal threesome since their freshman year of college. At the time of Rhoda's diagnosis, they both offered their total support. They understood, of course, that Rhoda felt angry and depressed, betrayed by her body, afraid of burdening others or being abandoned by them. Her friends listened to her, affirmed her feelings, and reassured her that she wouldn't be human if she could just put her fears out of her head. They were also tireless in helping her to get quality medical care.

After many remissions, plateaus, and flare-ups, it was soon clear that Rhoda was going rapidly downhill. Rhoda felt intense fear, grief, and anger each time her advancing illness caused new losses and challenges. "I'm not one of the lucky ones," she told me, referring to her doctor's comment that the disease was progressing much faster than he had anticipated. "Or," she added with a laugh, "I'm not even one of the lucky among the *un*lucky." And then, more somberly, "There's nothing lucky about getting any chronic illness."

## "It Is All Happening Perfectly!"

Two things brought Rhoda into therapy—her fear and grief about her illness, and a growing tension in her friendship with Barbara, the primary caretaker on the scene.

Rhoda told me that she and Barbara had once held similar "world views" about most things, including Rhoda's illness. At the time of the diagnosis, they had both cursed whatever combination of regrettable genes, environmental toxins, and bad luck had led to this outcome. They viewed her fall into illness as the result of a cosmic roll of the dice. Barbara, however, had since undergone "a spiritual shift." She now believed that everything happened for a reason, and was for the ultimate good. "It's all happening perfectly" was Barbara's new mantra. She was becoming, in Rhoda's words, "a mushy, born-again, New Age dolt."

When best friends grow apart in their core beliefs, it's always hard. Perhaps their strong friendship would have been able to accommodate this important difference were it not for the fact that Barbara was trying, with missionary zeal, to convince Rhoda to see things her way and adopt a more positive attitude. She told Rhoda that her fear, anger, and pessimism were making her condition worse, that she needed to rid herself of negative emotions in order to bolster her immune system, attract the positive energy of the universe, and live each day to the fullest.

Rhoda, for her part, resented the push to feel plucky and upbeat. She was also angry at Barbara's belief that we get what we deserve in some cosmic sense we may not be able to understand. "She's off in Woo-woo Land," Rhoda told me. Rhoda felt that Barbara was subtly blaming her for getting sick, although Barbara denied feeling that way. In any case, Rhoda was spending too much mental energy being angry at Barbara, when she needed that energy to get through the day.

## Pushing Positive Thinking

According to Rhoda, her interaction with Barbara went like this: She would tell Barbara how frightened and miserable she was, and then Barbara would tell her that she needed to stop feeding herself the negative thoughts that paralyzed her with fear. Barbara would then suggest things Rhoda could do, such as practicing positive affirmations. To this end, Barbara typed up the ones she thought would help Rhoda the most: "I am strong." "It's all part of the grand design." "I am a healing force in the universe." "I can handle all that happens in my life in a loving and powerful way." Barbara copied these from a bestselling book by Susan Jeffers called *Feel the Fear and Do It Anyway*, which Rhoda described as "Barbara's new Bible."

To Rhoda's dismay, for her birthday Barbara gave her the book along with a companion workbook by the same author. Barbara had highlighted choice parts in yellow, underlined key sentences in red, and inscribed it with "You can replace your negative thoughts with positive ones!" She cheerfully told Rhoda that the author had had a mastectomy after a breast cancer diagnosis and that cancer had been her wake-up call, allowing her to focus on simple pleasures like a hot shower or the first cup of coffee in the morning.

"This is so icky," Rhoda said to me during one session when she was in good humor. "It makes me think of that Stuart Smalley guy on *Saturday Night Live* who stands in front of the mirror and says, 'I'm good enough, I'm smart enough, and gosh darn it, people like me.' " Suffice it to say, Rhoda didn't respond well to Barbara's educational efforts.

Actually, Rhoda read the books and tried to be open to the idea that "We create our own reality." She read with interest the author's argument that positive words ("I am strong") make us physically and emotionally strong and that negative words ("I can't cope") make us physically and emotionally weak. She practiced the exercises in the book for several days, inspired by the author's argument that it doesn't matter if we believe what we're saying because the constant uttering of affirmations convinces the inner self.

But she didn't stick with it. In truth, Rhoda wasn't much of a positive thinker. The only sentence in the book that captured her rapt attention was one that Barbara had *not* underlined or highlighted. The author noted that it was important to "be around positive people." When Rhoda's eyes landed on these words, it suddenly dawned on her that her very worst fear was that Barbara would abandon her if she couldn't "get positive."

"Where is Evelyn in all this?" I asked her more than once.

"Evelyn agrees with me that Barbara is on a bandwagon, but she doesn't react to it the way I do. She says, 'Well, that's just Barbara.' "

I suggested to Rhoda that we invite Barbara and Evelyn to join us in therapy for a few sessions. After all, they were her family of choice, and there was a crisis in this family. Both women accepted the invitation. They loved Rhoda and they were deeply affected by what she was going through.

## Opening the Conversation

During the first meeting, I asked Barbara and Evelyn how they were doing since Rhoda's diagnosis. Evelyn said she wished she had time to be more available to Rhoda. Barbara said she was worried about Rhoda's fear and negativity.

Rhoda jumped right in and told Barbara that she resented feeling pressured to maintain a mood of cheerfulness. She had said this several times before, but never so forcefully because she depended on Barbara and was afraid of alienating her. This time the conversation went further.

"You're wanting me to put a positive spin on my illness to make it easier for *yourself*," Rhoda told Barbara with open emotion. "You and Evelyn are my best friends in the world. If I can't be real with you, I don't know what I'll do."

"We want you to be real," insisted Evelyn. "But we also want you to have some pleasure in your life, and some hope."

"Your negativity is wearing you down," Barbara said next. "It's not good for you." She paused and added, "It's wearing me down, too."

"Then stay away!" Rhoda snapped at Barbara. The anger in her voice betrayed the fact that she was inviting Barbara to do what Rhoda feared the most—abandon her.

"I'm not staying away!" Barbara snapped back. "I'm just upset because I'm doing everything to help you and you're not doing anything to help yourself!"

"How am I supposed to help myself with your magical thinking?" Rhoda shot back. "I'm dying, for God's sake. I'm falling apart before your eyes! And you want me to spend twenty minutes a day saying positive affirmations?"

"Positive thinking is more than that," Barbara replied. "You don't get it because you're not open to it." Suddenly Barbara began to cry. "I just can't stand to see this happen and feel so helpless!"

Evelyn, the quietest of the three, jumped in. "I feel that way, too, the helplessness part. I know this is really stupid . . ." she said, looking first at me and then at her friends. "Anna [her daughter] has this plastic magic wand she got at a science museum." Evelyn paused, looking so self-conscious that I wondered if she would proceed.

"Every day I walk around the house tapping the wand on the furniture saying, 'Get better Rhoda, get better Rhoda.'" Evelyn's eyes filled with tears. "I've tapped that stupid wand on everything in my house. I picture I'm tapping you on your head or on your shoulder saying, 'Get better Rhoda, get better Rhoda' and then suddenly you're totally healthy. There's no trace of the illness, it's all gone." She burst into tears.

Barbara said that she, too, kept imagining a magical cure. "Since college we've talked about being three old ladies together. I can't accept that won't happen."

"Well, I'm not even going to live long enough to get wrinkles," Rhoda said with a tough but warm edge. She had the only dry eyes in the room. "You'll just have to get used to the idea of being *two* old ladies together. And there's no guarantee of *that*, either."

Rhoda's humor and equanimity returned to her as her friends showed their own softness, vulnerability, fear, and concern. There was a palpable sense of relief and warmth in the room as a result of the frank and open conversation. They had given voice to their unspoken fears and, as a result, were in a position to manage them.

## Widening the Network of Helpers

What was especially painful for all three women to acknowledge was that they needed to get other people involved in Rhoda's care. Some of what needed to be done felt very private to Rhoda. Barbara and Evelyn were the only people she wanted on the scene. If everyone were healthy, it would be fine to be a tight threesome. It wasn't fine anymore. It was time to find additional help.

Of the two friends, Barbara was by far the more overwhelmed and exhausted, because she did most of what needed to be done for Rhoda. She lived within walking distance of Rhoda's house, worked out of a home office, and had no one else in her household. Evelyn, in contrast, lived twenty minutes away from Rhoda and had daughters, ages four and seven. Evelyn did a lot for Rhoda, but she was also protective of her own needs and those of her family. While Barbara's life was also full, she was the one who was always "on call."

Barbara feared she would devastate Rhoda by speaking the truth—that on some days she felt so desperate and depleted, she thought she'd have a nervous breakdown. She was exhausted by the practical and emotional demands of caretaking, and she was full of fear about what would happen as Rhoda's health declined and her needs increased. I teased Barbara that becoming mentally ill would be one way to communicate to Rhoda that there were limits to what she could give and do. Perhaps she could think of a less dramatic way to let her friend know when her caretaking limits had been exceeded.

We can only absorb so much anxiety without becoming sick or

symptomatic ourselves. Better for Barbara to lovingly define her limits than try to shape up Rhoda's attitude. Could Barbara learn to say, "I love you, but there are limits to what I can do"? And "I can't come over, I'm too exhausted." Could she hold her ground even if Rhoda protested that she didn't want strangers in her home, that her mother only made things worse, that Barbara and Evelyn were the only ones for the job, that no one else would do?

Barbara had trouble clarifying for herself, let alone to Rhoda, how much she could comfortably do or give. But she took on the challenge, knowing that nothing would get easier as Rhoda's health deteriorated and her needs increased. Rhoda quickly came to realize that while she would have a hard time relying less on Barbara, everyone would benefit if she widened her network of helpers.

## Changes That Make a Difference

Periodically, I saw the three women together. Each made positive changes. Barbara "got it" that her attempts to get Rhoda to think positively only left Rhoda feeling more alone and isolated with her fears. She learned to listen to Rhoda when she was suffering, to ask questions, to simply say, "I'm so sorry you have to deal with this." She offered Rhoda the gift of her full attention rather than a spiritual pep talk. Sometimes she would ask Rhoda what ideas she had to make her life a little easier, or she would suggest an idea of her own—but she didn't get back on her soapbox. Rhoda, for her part, began to truly appreciate the extent of her friend's emotional and physical exhaustion. She refrained from sharing her fear and hopelessness the minute Barbara stepped in the door.

Evelyn did many chores for Rhoda, but she didn't stay very long when she visited, partly because of family responsibilities, and partly because distance was her way of managing anxiety. In one of our sessions, she confessed another "secret," more difficult to tell than her magic wand ritual. Whenever she visited Rhoda, a heavy fatigue descended upon her, and she had to fight to keep her eyes open.

"I think it's about my girls," she said when I asked her how she understood her difficulty staying awake. "It's unbearable to think that something like this could happen to one of them. I don't mean to say that Rhoda is some kind of downer, but I can't stand being reminded that we're all so vulnerable, that nobody is safe."

Evelyn anxiously examined Rhoda's face to see how she was responding to this revelation. To Evelyn's surprise, Rhoda was unfazed. "Of course I'm a reminder that bad things happen." She took no offense at all. If anything, Evelyn's honesty and vulnerability made Rhoda feel closer to her.

"Why don't you lie down and sleep on my couch if you get so bone-tired?" Rhoda suggested. "Just show up—and sleep." Sometimes Evelyn did just that. As the mother of two small children, she was always tired anyway. Interestingly, her fatigue diminished now that she wasn't keeping it secret, and when flopping down on Rhoda's couch was an option.

"Nothing is more important than the people who care about you," Rhoda commented during one of our individual sessions. "Okay, then," I said to Rhoda. "So what about your mother?"

## A Crash Course in Assertiveness

When Rhoda first came to see me, her mother was denied "visitation rights" because she "hovered and smothered." Rhoda also said that although her mother came over to take care of her, Rhoda took care of her mother instead. Her mom's anxiety was so high that she constantly invited reassurance from Rhoda, and Rhoda gave it. ("There are a lot of smart researchers working on this, Mom.")

Of course, her mother's anxiety only increased with the enforced distance, which led her to do more of the "hovering behaviors" Rhoda found obnoxious. With my encouragement, Rhoda invited her mother for short visits and prepared herself in advance to let her mom know when she wasn't being helpful. Rhoda found that when she spoke up immediately, rather than letting her anger build, she felt better. And her mother was more open to hearing her when there was less intensity in Rhoda's voice.

On one weekend visit, for example, Rhoda's mother did her "moping, hovering, hand-wringing, poor-me, pity-pot thing," as Rhoda called it. I suggested we include her mother in a few sessions, but Rhoda didn't want to. "You'll have to accept my imitation of my mother," Rhoda said, as she proceeded with a dramatic flair: "Oh Rhoda, Rhoda, my poor Rhoda! If only I could take this illness from you. If only it were me that was sick and you were healthy. I would do anything to change places with you! Please God, please let me change places with my daughter. Oh, God, how could this happen to me."

I couldn't help but smile at Rhoda's imitation, which she insisted was not a caricature but "the real thing." I could also imagine the depths of her mother's pain.

"What did you say then?" I asked Rhoda.

Rhoda told me she was very straightforward. She said, "Mom, I know it's terrible to think about outliving your child. I can't begin to know how hard it is for you to watch me go through this. Believe me, it's hard for me to go through it. But you're acting like it's the end of the world, and that isn't helpful to me. I need you to focus more on what I need and less on how hard it is for you, even if you have to fake it."

"Oh my God," Rhoda said after reporting this conversation. "I can't believe how bossy I'm getting. I'm telling my mother what to do." She paused and said wisely, "But this is *my* illness, not hers. I have to tell her what I need."

Rhoda also began to feel more empathy for her mother during our work together. She saw her mother's self-centered behaviors more clearly—as an expression of pure anxiety. She asked her mother about other losses in her mom's family. As her mother talked about her own mother's early death at forty-seven, they shared a good cry, their arms around each other.

Rhoda learned to value the sharing of real feelings with her mother, while blocking her mother's undiluted, anxious reactivity, which left Rhoda feeling clenched up inside. She learned to pay attention when any conversation—be it with her mother or a neighbor—dampened her spirits, left her feeling down, or increased her anxiety. She learned to avoid such conversations, shift them to something else, or stop them early.

"I don't have that kind of time," she told me.

## The Challenge of Chronic Illness

There is nothing useful in drowning in fear and grief. Rhoda wanted to honor her suffering, while living her life as fully and wisely as possible. That is not only the challenge of chronic illness. It's the daily challenge for every person on the planet.

Interestingly, Rhoda became more positive in her outlook. She began to do things that made her feel better. One day Rhoda announced in therapy that she had had an epiphany about the importance of positive thinking— although not Barbara's particular brand of it. "Something hit me after our last therapy session," she told me. "I would never tell anybody *else* that she was pathetic, or couldn't cope, or that she was weak, marked for tragedy, and too disgusting to be part of this beautiful world. And I would not hang around with anyone who said these things to me. So why am I saying these things to myself? Of course I'm more likely to believe these things if I keep saying them to myself!"

She declared that she would not spend her limited time with thoughts that added an extra layer of suffering to the real pain she was coping with. She began to understand, in her own way, how powerful the mind is, how our thoughts make us feel better or worse. She started to practice meditation for twenty minutes a day, and she gathered additional resources to manage her fear as well as possible. Biofeedback, massage, music, breathing techniques, and psychotherapy all helped her. So did an antidepressant and the occasional Valium or Ativan. Her connections to people who cared about her were most helpful of all.

Rhoda created a team of healers, including authors and experts she would never meet, but whose wisdom touched her deeply. She especially appreciated books and tapes by authors who had experienced chronic or terminal illness, disability, and loss. She wasn't drawn to tips or techniques for managing fear and grief. She found it most helpful to read the firsthand experiences of people who had "been there." She also got a computer fitted for her disability, and over the Internet communicated with others living with similar degenerative neuromuscular disorders. She realized that she was not alone, that she was traveling in wonderful company, and that hearing other people's stories opened up her heart.

## The Power of Pretending

Sometimes the best thing Rhoda could do with her suffering was to suffer. She chose to face her fear and grief, to go to the center of it, to observe it move through her body, to let it be, and to give voice to it. Nothing was more important to Rhoda than being around people with whom she could truly be herself.

But by paying careful attention to what left her feeling better or worse, Rhoda also learned the power of pretending and the benefits of distracting herself from fear and pain. Sometimes she would bravely put on a front and force herself to have visitors when she didn't feel like it, or she would smile and act happy when she felt dreadful. She discovered that acting "as if" lifted her spirits and that pretending to feel joy or courage evoked her capacity for it.

While it's important to feel capable of sharing fear and sorrow, creative pretending can sometimes be a helpful way of lightening our burden, of getting back in touch with our capacity for humor and enjoyment, no matter how harrowing the times.

## "I Am a Child of God"

Rhoda announced during a therapy session that she found herself an affirmation or mantra. It was "I am a child of God."

"Really?" I said. "You, Rhoda, the militant atheist?" I could not have been more surprised. "How did this come to you?"

"I'm not sure, but I think I heard Maya Angelou say it on television," Rhoda replied. "I say it when I look in the mirror every morning, and it makes me smile. Just repeating it to myself makes me realize the truth of it."

"What is the truth of it to you?" I asked.

"It's not about God in the usual sense of a grave old man with a long beard," Rhoda explained, "but when I connect to these words, I feel that I'm part of the vast universal family, the flow of life." She explained that whenever she started to feel isolated, alien, and different or marked, she says, "I am a child of God."

"Automatically these words make me smile," Rhoda said. "I feel loved or I let love in."

Rhoda paused for a moment and looked at me sheepishly. "Okay, go ahead and say it. I'm turning into a mushy New Age dolt, aren't I?"

•  •  •

There was nothing easy for Rhoda about having her young body lose its functioning at warp speed, to so quickly come to a place where she couldn't lift a spoon of cereal to her mouth. In the time left to her, she had nightmares, moments of terror, fear, rage, envy, and grief. Sometimes she was cranky, irritable, and distracted when people tried to help her.

She also had many wonderful days and moments. She managed her illness and dying process with dignity, by which I do not mean that she "looked good," avoided diapers, or conducted herself with equanimity, grace, and good cheer. I mean that she kept growing, stayed connected with the people who loved her, and made an effort to live to the full extent of her possibilities. She learned to be more openhearted with her mother and other family members. She tried to be a "good Buddhist," as she referred to her moderately successful efforts to open herself to the present moment rather than clouding that moment with thoughts about what should be or what could have been. Rhoda never stopped being funny, even about death.

Barbara and Evelyn spoke at Rhoda's funeral. Each shared what they had learned from her. Barbara said, "She taught me how to listen, to really listen rather than trying to control things—a gift I will always treasure."

Evelyn said, "She taught me that nothing is more important than showing up."

A month before Rhoda died, she said she wanted a "splendid funeral," with no false sentimentality. She got it. It was a packed house, a profoundly moving service. She would have approved.

## CULTIVATING PERSPECTIVE

When bad things happen (which they will), you can both honor your fear and suffering, and also learn how to direct your attention away from it. You can find a way to connect more to the human family, as Rhoda did with the words, "I am a child of God" and Lindbergh did with the mustard seed story. You can learn to stop comparing yourself to others, which will only keep you riveted on the unfairness of life.

You can have better quality of life each day if you practice focusing on what you still have. You are terminally ill, but you love the quality of light that comes through the window. You can no longer walk the trail, but you can sit outside and smell the night air. You have friends and relatives you love and value. The worst has happened, but you can watch the insects and birds do their work. There is still pleasure in what is near at hand.

Many clients have told me that writing "a gratitude list" every night is a helpful ritual. "I can hear the music." "I have a cat who loves me no matter what." "I can see the sky today." Too often, what goes well goes unnoticed. Jon Kabat-Zinn observes, "Your lack of a headache is not front-page news for your cerebral cortex." But we can learn to use fear, pain, and grief to bring the "ordinary" into focus.

Many folks in decent health are quite certain they want to be pushed off a cliff as soon as they lose their independence and "quality of life." The day comes when this happens, and they may discover simple pleasures and the wish to see another day. "Whee!" says the snail riding on the turtle's back! Everything is a matter of perspective.

## An Act of Grace

One of the many ways people achieve perspective is through a connection to nature. My mother, Rose, was terrified when she was diagnosed with metastatic cancer at forty-seven because she was convinced I couldn't grow up okay without her. I was twelve at the time, and in a variety of trouble. "I can't die," I heard her tell some-one on the phone. "Harriet is such a mess."

I never thought of my mother as having had an especially deep connection to the natural world, but she was profoundly affected by visiting the Grand Canyon after her radiation treatments were over. A reassuring sense of her smallness and insignificance enveloped her. If she died, she died. I'd grow up one way or another. What would be would be. Instead of feeling daunted by her comparatively small place in the universe, she found it comforting to remember the vastness and mysteriousness of life and death. There is peace in let-ting go.

The peace that came over her settled in and stayed. When she got back to Brooklyn, fear shaped her life with a far lighter hand. She also listened to fear in order to act wisely. She made plans for me to stay with her brother Bo and his family in Brooklyn in the case of her death. She knew, and rightly so, that my father would not be able to begin to take care of me on his own.

My mother experienced what some would call transcendence or "spiritual detachment." This is a place you cannot "choose" but can only find in yourself. Paradoxically, detachment comes hand-in-hand with the capacity to be most fully alive and open to what-ever is. The late writer Philip Simmons, diagnosed with ALS (Lou Gehrig's disease) at age thirty-five, speaks of this paradox—this in-separable combination of living fully and letting go. He calls this "learning to fall," the title of the book he wrote after becoming ill.

> . . . we deal most fruitfully with loss by accepting the fact that we will one day lose everything. When we learn to fall, we learn that only by letting go our grip on all that we ordi-narily find most precious—our achievements, our plans, our loved ones, our very selves—we can find, ultimately, the most profound freedom.

The "art of falling," or however you name it, sometimes comes through hard-earned, dedicated, daily meditative or spiritual practice. Sometimes, as my mother did, we find it by an act of grace. Either way, it begins with an acknowledgment of our inability to control the circumstances of life and death. My mother, as it turned out, lived to be ninety-four years old. Her brother Bo, however, was killed in a car accident in his fifties. Death cares very little for our predictions or plans.

## CREATIVE COPING

How do you calm down, gain perspective, and have the best quality of life each day? What helps people is as different as the people who need help. Staying open to every resource you find is good, because some of the things that help you deal with catastrophe—or just plain stress—may take you by surprise. A client of mine discovered following a heart attack that he had a deep capacity for prayer. He never suspected that he had a gift for finding peace in this particular activity. Another client who couldn't stand any of "that Buddhist, be-here-now, Eastern stuff" found that meditation helped her the most when her daughter got sick.

There are so many things we can choose to do that help us to have a better life. In her book *Letters to a Young Therapist*, Mary Pipher writes like a woman in love when she describes her relationship to swimming, and how it awakens, heals, relaxes, and rejuvenates her. In water she solves her thorniest problems and revisits the happiest events. Commenting on the "primordial nature" of this activity, she writes: "We are made of water, once long ago we lived in water, and with swimming we return to water." And more simply, "I don't think anything beats swimming."

I sent Pipher's reflections on swimming to a friend in Cleveland who was awash with anxiety after divorcing and losing her job in the same year. My friend, a self-avowed "Mary Pipher fan" swam competitively in high school, but hadn't been in water for more than a decade. Swimming had once been "her thing" and, as I predicted, she resonated with Pipher's enthusiasm. "But it's fifteen minutes for me to get to the pool," she told me, "and with changing and showering it takes up too much time. Plus, I don't like running into people in a bathing suit, the way I look. No way I'm going to swim now." Ditto for hiking or dancing or getting a massage or anything else that might help her to feel better.

Nothing will help you if you don't have the motivation to act. You can't be like the person who lies in bed shivering, but won't get up to get another blanket because he tells himself he's too tired. Most of us seek help from experts when we haven't begun to do the things we know we need to do for ourselves.

Then there's that small matter of discipline. Just about anything really worth doing requires motivation, courage, and the willingness to practice. It helps to break a goal into small steps and take the first one. A writer friend from Oskaloosa, Kansas, Lou Ann Thomas, described herself as dangerously overweight when she received a breast cancer diagnosis at the age of forty-six. She was terrified and decided to start paying attention to her health. She had lost 190 pounds when I saw her last, some years postdiagnosis. "I couldn't fathom losing 100 or 150 pounds, and never in my wildest imagination could I picture losing 190," she wrote, "but I knew I could lose one pound. That was doable, achievable and possible, so I simply lost one pound 190 times."

A crisis can become an opportunity to live more fully and healthfully, or to make some bold and courageous act of change in an important relationship. Things fall apart, and we vow to begin to live more mindfully, with careful attention to what is. If we stay on automatic pilot, we live less in the present than in the past and future—

like the bumper sticker that says, "Having a good time, wish I were here." A crisis can knock us awake.

A crisis, however, can also be the most difficult time to direct our attention to the beauty of the moment or to enhance a relationship we never worked on to begin with. Crises evoke anxiety, which, by its nature, drives worry and rumination and sets your brain on overdrive. We are better able to deal with tragedy if we've already begun the process of coming to terms with the unpredictability and unfairness of life in our calmer moments.

Why wait for the universe to send you a great big lesson in fear, vulnerability, and loss? We can all move in the direction of more peacefulness and authentic connection with neighbors, friends, and family, rather than moving in the direction of more distance and isolation. We can each look for our personal mustard seed story, a fitting mantra, and ways to calm ourselves and live more lovingly and mindfully.

## CHAPTER 11

# Courage in the Face of Fear

Without courage to draw upon, we let fear, anxiety, and shame overshadow our best selves. Our lives become narrow, our hearts small. "Life shrinks or expands in proportion to one's courage," Anais Nin wrote. How true. Nothing is more important than courage.

But what *is* courage? In a world saturated with images of action-figure bravado, we may mistakenly believe that courage is the absence of fear. Instead, it is the capacity to think, speak, and act *despite* our fear and shame.

Throughout this book, we've seen many examples of everyday courage and what it requires of us. I invite you to consider how you define courage in your own life and how you might practice more of it. Everything in this world that is truly worth doing takes practice. Courage is no exception.

## WHAT COURAGE IS *NOT*

When I was growing up, I thought that being courageous meant not being afraid. Similarly, I thought cowardice meant fear. By these false definitions I was both brave and cowardly depending on when and where you peeked in on my life.

As a young adult, for example, I was good at fearlessness. I spent my junior year of college in India, inspired by my best friend, Marla, who was majoring in Indian studies. Once there, I threw caution to the wind. When Marla and I were in Nepal and she proposed that we trek to a remote village, I was game. No matter that this village, a day trip from our point of departure in Katmandu, could only be reached by horseback. No matter that I had only a brief stint of riding experience from one month of summer camp and Marla had none. No matter that our guide spoke only Nepalese while we spoke only a little Hindi, and poorly at that. We lost him after a couple of hours anyway, or maybe he just went home. That we lived to tell of this adventure is a small miracle.

Because I was young, I didn't think tragedy or death could touch me. I didn't even take illness all that seriously. While abroad I was diagnosed with a long list of diseases, including malaria and amoebic dysentery, which I thought made me a more interesting person. I thought my own mother was ridiculous for worrying about me when I wrote home about my funny adventures, like stepping out of a cab in Goa in the middle of the night into a six-foot ditch where I was bitten by a poisonous snake. Why was she such a worrywart?

I had no clue that a decade later, motherhood would turn me into a champion worrier. Having children taught me all about fear, and suddenly life was a wolf prowling outside the door ready to pounce on my children when I wasn't paying attention. In fact, if you looked in on my more anxious moments of parenting, you might wonder whatever happened to that intrepid young woman in India. You could only conclude that she had been abducted by aliens and replaced by some other person whose brain went to worst-case scenarios like a moth to a flame.

Was I a courageous person when I was a student, and a coward after my kids came along? Not at all. I simply experienced anxiety differently at different points in the life cycle. When I was younger, I denied danger. After my first child was born, I developed an over-reactive fear response, at least as far as survival anxiety was concerned. I wish my neural circuitry had been more easygoing while I was rearing my children. But that's how it was.

## THE TRUE MEANING OF BRAVERY

Fearlessness, as enviable as you may find it, is not the same as courage, which requires you to act when you are afraid or uncomfortable. We are all brave in some ways and not in others. There are an infinite number of ways a person can act with courage, or fail to, on a particular day. What constitutes courage is rarely the heroic deeds that action and adventure films are made of.

Don't assume that your best friend who is preparing to climb Mount Kilimanjaro lives more courageously than your neighbor who spends every vacation puttering around her house and garden. The person who stays close to home may indeed be living a small, fear-driven life. Alternatively, her relationship to home and place may be marvelously complex and filled with experiments in the kitchen, workshop, and garden that require an adventurous spirit. Maybe she takes courageous political stands or takes risks in her personal relationships that are hard for her, that make her afraid, and she does them anyway. And maybe your adventurous, risk-taking friend is totally unable to find her voice to talk with her parents about things that trouble her, ask for help when she needs it, or engage openly in questioning, criticism, and dissent on issues that matter to her.

Private, invisible acts of courage are not apparent to others. And what constitutes a courageous act will not be the same for two people, or even for the same person on a different day. In one circumstance, courage might mean giving vent to the full measure of your anger. In a different situation, you may need to muster every molecule of courage to open a difficult conversation in a kind and temperate way when you want to come out with guns blazing.

We can't evaluate courage from the outside because courage comes from the inside. For example, I recently conducted an evening program on anger at a women's prison, and some sensitive issues between the prisoners and the prison staff came out in the open. When I described the experience to a friend, she exclaimed, "Harriet, you are so brave!" In fact, I was feeling extremely brave that night and rightfully proud, if I do say so myself.

My courageous act was driving myself to the facility after dark, even though I had never been there before and could have gotten someone else to take me. The program I conducted on women's anger, by contrast, didn't evoke any particular anxiety or require me to push against resistance. Finding my way to an unfamiliar place at night, when decades of avoidance had led to near-paralysis at the mere thought of doing so, was truly brave for me.

Courage, to me, has several elements. First, you need to clarify your authentic goals, values, beliefs, and directions. Perhaps your intuition tells you to sign up for a dance class, or to initiate more contact with your brother, or to revisit a painful issue with your mother. Perhaps your intention is to create a better marriage. Then you need to act—and stay on course—even when you meet with the inevitable resistance from within and without. Let's look at some examples.

## TO SPEAK OR NOT TO SPEAK

In 1972 I moved to Topeka, Kansas, to do a postdoctoral fellowship at the Menninger Foundation, where I subsequently joined the staff. I was the sole feminist in this large psychiatric center (or more accurately, the only person back then who used the f-word). In my previous life in Berkeley, and before that in New York, feminism was flourishing around me, but I didn't get it. Looking back, I must have been sleepwalking, or perhaps in a coma. But once ensconced in a conservative psychoanalytic institution in Topeka, necessity became the mother of comprehension. I got it.

Here in the land of patriarchy, I took it upon myself to speak up whenever I saw unfairness and injustice, especially as it affected the understanding and treatment of women. This meant that I was speaking up all the time, and I was basically alone on the job. Not surprisingly, I soon became stuck in the role of "Foundation Feminist," and I lost my capacity to be heard. It was like, "Oh no, there she goes again." I also dissipated an incredible amount of energy trying to inform and enlighten my senior colleagues, which, in retrospect, is a project akin to trying to change your parents.

It was courageous of me to say what I believed and act on my principles, sometimes at significant personal cost. But simply voicing anger and protest didn't require the large measure of courage it appeared to, because it's just what I automatically do. I move quickly to the center of difficult emotional issues, and when I feel passionately about something I may make my case for the forty-ninth time, just in case the other person didn't get it the first forty-eight times. Conflict is usually not difficult for me. On the contrary, I am most anxious and uncomfortable when I want to speak, or believe I should speak, and choose not to.

## "Don't Just Do Something! Stand There!"

Courage for me in the workplace required that I experiment with *not* speaking up. It made me quite uncomfortable to refrain from saying the tempting thing at the wrong moment, and to go the hard route of thoughtfully deciding how and when to say what to whom. It took courage to clarify for myself what I really wanted to accomplish in my work setting, and to know when to be strategic rather than spontaneous in accomplishing difficult goals.

What were some of my courageous acts of silence? Unfair criticism and being "unappreciated" were emotional triggers for me, and my automatic tendency was to jump in to argue what was true and who was right. For me, it took enormous courage to practice pure listening, which meant listening only to understand another person's negative feedback. I would first apologize for the piece I could wrap my brain around, even if it was embedded in exaggeration and misunderstanding. Only then would I state my own point of view—without defensiveness and without blaming the person who criticized me.

I also stopped addressing every injustice and took a clear stand only on issues that mattered most to me. I learned to "strike when the iron is cold." At the very moment I felt like strangling the other person I would say, "I need a little time to sort my thoughts out. Let's set up another time to talk about this." I tried to underreact and take a low-key approach in emotionally loaded situations. This made for calmer work relationships, since anxiety and intensity are the driving forces behind dysfunctional, downward-spiraling patterns. When in the grip of strong emotions in the workplace, my mantra became the reversal of an old maxim: "Don't just do something. Stand there!"

Bold acts of courage, personally and politically, require a commitment to acting wisely and well. You don't just hold your nose, close your eyes, and jump. Sometimes courageous acts of change need to be plotted, strategized, and planned. Choosing silence over speech, so that I could become a more effective agent of change, took all my courage.

## The Costs of Silence

Sam, a psychiatrist friend of mine, faced the opposite challenge in his organization on the East Coast. He was high up in the hierarchy of a major psychoanalytic institute and had some clout to change things, but his anxiety silenced him. When stress hit, his automatic style was to become conciliatory, conflict-avoidant, and accommodating. He resisted voicing ideas that would make him the target of other people's anger or disapproval.

His work system was his "family," and he was afraid to threaten his inside position in the group by voicing dissent. For example, Sam was developing a keen interest in spirituality as it applied to the process of psychoanalysis. Fearing that his more conservative and scientifically minded colleagues would disapprove, he kept these ideas to himself. He worried about harming his credibility by being seen as flaky.

Shame also silenced him, not that Sam ever used that word. But shame lurks beneath our social fears and concerns about our own adequacy. In his work setting, as in mine, a premium was placed on being highly articulate. A number of professionals on staff spoke with such eloquence and wit that Sam told me he often wanted to write their words down and read them over simply for pleasure. But that was their gift, not his. Sam's gift was, among other things, his limber, creative brain.

The higher Sam climbed in the organization, the more risky it felt to share a half-formulated thought at a meeting, or to speak without being "well-spoken." Increasingly, he held back until his thoughts were crystal-clear and finalized—which meant he rarely spoke at all. He once told me he wished he had published when he was young, as I did, because he had waited too long. "What is too long?" I inquired. Sam explained that any publication he'd put out now, as a senior psychiatrist, would have to be "significant"—an expectation that blocked him from writing at all.

Sam, by his own account, wanted to be a more adventurous, authentic spirit. He would tell me how formal his colleagues were, and how he longed to be part of a relaxed, creative "think tank" where people could brainstorm without having to worry about sounding less than brilliant. Sometimes Sam talked about leaving his job and joining friends in a private practice group in Palo Alto. But he didn't leave, and he didn't risk speaking up in the only workplace he knew.

Sam articulated other fears that we can all resonate with—the fear of not being good enough, of not living life productively and creatively, of not "succeeding" in a meaningful, authentic way. He would often tell his own therapy clients that the journey of life involves forging one's own path and not merely falling in line with a sort of mass consensus about what that path should look like. But Sam let fear and shame stop him from fully moving forward on his own journey.

More accurately, Sam's avoidance of these emotions was the problem. Sam didn't experiment with new behaviors that might have evoked fear and shame, so he didn't learn he could feel these emotions and cope. Courage requires us to face such uninvited guests, because they predictably show up with new territory. The effort to *avoid* discomfiting emotions drains our courage.

A postscript: Sam, now in his mid-sixties, has retired from his organization and is working on a book on spirituality. While he tells me how great it feels to be doing his own work in his own way, he also is aware of lost chances, the quickening of time. He realizes that had he stood up to his fear early on and spoken his truth to his conservative colleagues, he would have begun to "be the person I really am" much sooner. As author Martha Beck reminds us, fear is the constant companion of everyone who is living his destiny.

## STANDING UP TO POWER

Finding your voice in an unequal power arrangement—especially when the more powerful person is shaming you—takes a great amount of courage. Consider my client Margot, whom I first met when she was a high school senior, full of talent and energy, with a huge gift for empathy and connection. She also was vulnerable to deep depression and would later be diagnosed with bipolar disorder. During her freshman year of college, she made a suicide attempt after a boyfriend broke up with her. Needless to say, it was the year from hell for Margot, and terrifying for her family who loved her.

When Margot returned home over spring break, she visited her favorite teacher in high school, a man who had mentored her and believed in her promise. After some catch-up conversation, the teacher said, "I was so sorry to hear about your suicide attempt, Margot. To be frank, I felt very disappointed. I didn't see you as the sort of person who would do such a thing." When they parted, the teacher gave her a hearty pat on the back and said, "I miss the *old* Margot. I know that strong gal is still in there somewhere!"

Margot had suffered enough, and was struggling mightily in her brief therapy with me to keep sight of her competence and strengths. She felt flattened by these words from a teacher who had once shown her the greatest attention and respect. Now, as he shamed her for her apparent "weakness," he invited Margot to see herself as "the sort of person who would do such a thing." What sort of person is that? And what did he mean by "such a thing"?

Plus, there was no "old" or "new" Margot. There was only Margot. She felt like a truck had hit her.

This eighteen-year-old girl, whose self-esteem was already badly bruised, wrote this teacher a note letting him know how badly this interaction had left her feeling. Her first draft was a long rant in which she vented her anger and cited extensive findings from the research literature on suicide. If Margot's intention were only to show her teacher the full force of her feelings—and to shame him in return—this letter would have done the job. But as I questioned Margot in therapy, she clarified that her primary intention was to make this teacher understand that he had no right to talk to her in such a hurtful and insensitive way.

Of course, we can't "make" other people understand anything or feel bad for their misdeeds. But given Margot's intention, this long, emotionally intense letter would simply have let the teacher off the hook. Unless he was a very highly evolved person, he would surely have reacted with defensiveness. When we blame the blamer (or shame the shamer), that person will wrap himself up in a blanket of rationalization and denial, and avoid feeling accountable. Also, people on the defensive rarely read long, critical letters, so I often coach people to "say it shorter." I doubted if Margot's teacher would do more than casually eyeball such a detailed critique.

Margot took a more courageous route by sending him a three-paragraph letter that he could not so easily disqualify or put aside. She wrote:

> You've been such an important person in my life. I came back to see you needing your support. It hurt me to be told that I've disappointed you, as if I'm some kind of failure. I left your office feeling like I was a smaller person, who didn't live up to your standards. Maybe that's what you believe, but it didn't help me to hear it. I also need to tell you that I don't

believe that I am a lesser person because of my suicide attempt.

In this bold note, Margot offered her teacher the opportunity to consider his behavior, to take responsibility for it, and to apologize. She left open the possibility of healing the disconnection between them, which made sense given how important he had been to her. To his credit, he called Margot at home and apologized, explaining that his insensitivity came out of his own anxiety about losing her and the fact that several years earlier, another student had committed suicide during her freshman year of college.

That this teacher rose to the occasion is far less important than that Margot wrote the letter. How incredibly brave for a young woman just out of high school, recovering from a major depression and the near loss of her life, to talk back to such an important authority—to let him know that she would not accept his invitation to view her suicide attempt and vulnerability to severe depression as shameful, lesser, weak, or wrong.

Courage is not blasting or blaming people, cutting them off, or parachuting from afar for dramatic, hit-and-run confrontations. Just the opposite. Genuine courage is carefully planning how to invite the person who has harmed you back into the conversation, so that the two of you have the best chance of talking together over time in a real way. This is the hard route Margot took, the path that evokes far more anxiety than venting emotion in an uncensored, reactive way.

## FEAR IS NOT THE PROBLEM

If you pay attention, you may find that it is not fear that stops you from doing the brave and true thing in your daily life. Rather, the problem is avoidance. You want to feel comfortable, so you avoid doing the thing that will evoke fear and other disquieting emotions.

Avoidance will make you feel less vulnerable in the short run, but it will never make you less afraid.

## When Habits Become Cables

Avoidance can be directed to particular objects, like cars, green parrots, or crowds. Or we may avoid particular challenges, like opening an anxious conversation and saying something the other person doesn't want to hear. But avoidance can also become a lifestyle.

Jill, for example, was thirty-one years old and married when she told me during our first session that she was "afraid of everything." On closer examination, she realized that she never let fear in the door—and *that* was her problem. As she described it, "When I put myself in a new situation like yoga class, it's like there is a magnet pulling me back to my own house where I'm comfortable." She added pensively, "No sooner do I arrive in a new place than I'm figuring out how to leave."

A Chinese proverb tells us that habits start out as silken threads that slowly, invisibly thicken and harden into cables. Jill held so tightly to the habitual that the habitual tightened its grip on her. She avoided even the slightest departure from her fixed routine. It was hard for her to remember the last time she ventured into a new opportunity for learning without scrambling back to the safety of the familiar. In therapy, Jill began to practice tolerating anxiety and discomfort. She changed the route of her daily walk, ordered an unfamiliar dish at a restaurant, and, most boldly, traveled to London with her girlfriend, although she struggled with the impulse to cancel every day leading up to the trip. Jill intentionally brought on the anxiety she needed to practice feeling by opening herself to new possibilities.

When Jill first came into therapy, she avoided the discomfiting emotions by staying within the confines of the comfortable. She hoped that I could help her to "become less anxious." As we've seen from earlier examples in this book, courage requires us to become *more* anxious in situations that we have previously avoided. By courageously pushing herself beyond her safety zone, Jill began to create a newly spacious life.

## One Size Doesn't Fit All

We all struggle to find the right balance between our human need for security, comfort, and predictability on the one hand, and our need for risk taking and growth on the other. In finding this balance, no single formula fits all—or even fits a particular individual over time. As always, getting stuck in the anxiety-driven extremes is problematic.

At one extreme, we may want to do nothing that threatens the status quo. The need for sameness, safety, and predictability may rule all our days and choices. If we—or a family member—move "too far" (be it geographically or in beliefs and choices), we may experience this shift as deeply threatening or disloyal. We may seek safety in the totally patterned and habitual, as Jill did at the start of therapy, as though we can deny that life is always process, movement, and transformation, and that nothing ever stays the same or lasts forever.

The other extreme is equally problematic. We may opt for the new and different because we are anxious about putting down roots and testing our capacity for deepening a connection to another person, project, or place. We may avoid making or honoring commitments. We may be comfortable with beginnings—but only with beginnings. We may deny the reality that what we hold most dear requires protection, and that authentic courage may require us to restrain from running off in a compelling new direction.

## ORDINARY COURAGE

Over three decades as a psychotherapist, I have watched people act with enormous bravery. Women and men feel fear, and they do the right thing. Or they don't feel the fear until *after* they start doing the right thing, but still they persist.

To many observers, the following actions might not appear heroic—or even especially noteworthy. No one rushed into a burning building. No one opened up a deeply painful subject like abuse or neglect with a family member. No one took a principled position that might cost him or her a relationship or a job. Nonetheless, these behaviors required the courage to experiment with bold new behaviors when there was a powerful pull to stay with habitual, safe old ways.

- In the middle of an intense marital fight, a wife suddenly stops arguing and tells herself that for the rest of the conversation, she will simply ask questions and try to understand her husband's point of view. She shifts into a place of pure listening, detaching from the question of who is right or what is true or how she can best make her case.

- A man, in the midst of a painful divorce, shares his vulnerability with his racquetball partner, whom he knows is also divorced. It is the first time he has revealed something personal to a male friend.

- A man arranges to take two days off work when his mother visits, instead of assuming that his wife will entertain her. He arranges a day trip for just the two of them and gets to know his mother better.

- A woman takes a bottom-line position with her chronically critical husband. She says, "I love you and I want to be your partner. But I can't listen when you approach me this way. You need to approach me with respect, or I won't be in the conversation." She sticks to her position over time, refusing to continue a conversation at her own expense.

- A husband tells his wife at breakfast, "I was thinking about the conversation we had last night." He then says, "I was wrong," and "I'm sorry." The last time he said these words to her were . . . well, he can't remember.

I help people practice courage in any context they dare to. If I led wilderness treks and outdoor adventures, like my intrepid psychologist friend Marilyn Mason, I'm sure I would be more attuned to different aspects of courage—the courage to prepare for a difficult mountain climb, the courage to keep climbing when you're scared or tired, the courage to trust yourself and your fellow travelers, the courage to honor your fear and limitations by saying, "I can't continue. I need to go back down the mountain." Given my own professional interests, I pay careful attention to relational courage—the courage to observe and change oneself in key relationships.

## COURAGE: LET ME COUNT THE WAYS

While we often think of courage as an individual act of bravery, there are also "categories" of courage to which we might aspire. Here's my short list:

*There is courage in taking action.* We take on a new challenge we prefer to avoid. We get on a plane, apply for a job, buy a bicycle, study for the GED, put aside time in the morning to write, take a Spanish class.

*There is courage in speaking.* We voice our differences, we share real feelings, we address a painful emotional issue, open a family secret, tell the truth. We take a clear position on things that matter to us. We clarify the limits of what we can or can't do. We speak not with the intention of getting comfortable but with the intention of being our best selves, even though we may be shaking in our boots.

*There is courage in questioning.* We ask questions about anxious emotional issues in our family history. We ask our partner questions that will allow us to know him or her more fully. When people we love have suffered, we invite them to tell us their stories, no matter how painful, rather than communicating that we don't want to hear it, or don't want to hear all of it. We ask, "Is there more you'd like to share?"

*There is courage in pure listening.* We practice listening with an open heart, and with the intention only to understand. We listen without defensiveness, and without the need to fix, instruct, or change the other person. We mindfully choose silence over speech, and resist saying the wrong thing at the tempting moment.

*There is courage in thinking for ourselves.* We clarify our own beliefs separate from what our family, friends, partner, therapist, workplace, or president tell us is right and true. We resist the pressure for a "group think" mentality even when we stand all alone with our perceptions, opinions, and beliefs.

*There is courage in being accountable.* We truly accept responsibility for our own less-than-honorable behaviors, even when doing so challenges our favored image of the self.

Other ideas or images of courage may occur to you. The courage to love and to create. The courage to know another person and be known. The courage to see yourself clearly. The courage to bring more of your authentic self into a relationship. The courage to be generous and patient. The courage to have an open mind. The courage to have an open heart. The courage to live your own life (not someone else's) as well as possible. The courage to honor a commitment. The courage to endure when something terrible happens to you or a family member. The courage of heroism in the usual sense, that is, the willingness to sacrifice everything because you believe so strongly in something. The courage to get through the day.

Sometimes, the most courageous thing you can do is simply to sit with unclarity and confusion for as long as you need to, resisting pressures from others to speak or act before you are ready. When you are ready, courage may require you to act in ways that elicit the fear or discomfort you believe you can't sit with—and then you learn that you *can*. It's the anxiety we don't name, try to avoid, or pass along to others that closes our hearts, distorts our thinking, and limits our possibilities of living more courageously. As the mystery writer Sue Grafton put it, "If you're not afraid, you're not trying hard enough."

## EXTRAORDINARY COURAGE: FACING SHAME

We've seen how paralyzing and debilitating shame can be, how it invites us to not be seen or heard, at least not in an authentic way. Acting courageously when shame enters the picture, as Margot did, requires extraordinary courage—because people will do anything to escape from shame, or from the possibility that shame will be evoked in a particular situation. It's just too difficult to "go there," even for people who will walk into the fires of transformation to face fear.

While there are countless exceptions to the rule, men and women tend to manage shame differently. Generally, men have less tolerance for shame, perhaps because they are shamed almost from birth for half their humanity—the so-called feminine part of themselves, including any vulnerable or "weak" feelings or behaviors.

Men often sit with shame for only a nanosecond before flipping it into something more "masculine" and therefore tolerable, like anger or rage, or a need to dominate, devalue, or control.

Bombs are dropped, innocent people are killed, and homes become unsafe for women and children when shame and fear come together in the masculine psyche. All too readily, shame can metamorphose into aggression and the wish for revenge. Meanwhile, fear causes a narrowing of perspective, an erasure of the broader history, a narrow focus on "who started it" from an all-good vs. all-evil mentality. Again, it's not the *experience* of fear and shame that makes terrible things happen in realms both personal and political. Rather, terrible things happen when people desperately and mindlessly try to avoid, or rid themselves, of these painful emotions.

Women can also flip shame into aggression and domination. But more frequently, women tend to take shame on, internalize it, and, as a result, feel deeply flawed, painfully disconnected, ugly, or disempowered. In the face of shame, it takes extraordinary courage to act wisely and well on one's own behalf. Bella's story illustrates how being shamed can easily pull a woman into passivity and inaction— but also how she can get "unstuck" by acting on her authentic feelings and beliefs.

## A Happy High School Reunion

Bella, a therapy client, was planning to attend her tenth high school reunion in a small city in Missouri. In preparation for the big celebration, participants were asked to submit a paragraph summarizing "life since high school" for a newsletter that would be mailed in advance to all the attendees. Bella mentioned her marriage, her journalism degree, her farm animals, and the grief of losing her daughter, Anna, who had died from meningitis when she was four months and ten days old.

When Bella received her copy of the newsletter in the mail, she was stunned to see that what she had written about Anna had been omitted. She called the woman in charge of organizing the reunion, and was passed from one person to another before she finally connected with a school administrator who gave her an explanation. A "consensus" had been reached, he explained, to not include material that could disturb other classmates.

Fired by anger and indignation, Bella argued that this was her life, that it was true and real and what had actually happened to her. She also told the administrator that from her journalistic perspective, this was censorship and from a human perspective it simply wasn't right, to say nothing of the fact that nobody had even paid her the courtesy of telling her that the material about her daughter would be cut. It took great courage for Bella to say this much. She was a shy person.

This man was not listening, not really, and he continued to shame her. "Of course, you should feel free to tell anybody whatever you please at the reunion," he assured her. "But there is no need to put your private pain in print. The reunion is a celebration, and we want everyone to attend in this spirit."

By the time I saw Bella in therapy, her anger had dissolved into tearful helplessness, and her shame felt larger than one room could contain. Between wrenching sobs, she told me that she was definitely *not* going to the reunion. Now she imagined her classmates pitying her or gossiping about her if she talked about Anna. Yet what was the point of going if she couldn't talk about what was real?

Still weeping, Bella told me she hated herself, that she had failed at the most important thing in the world—keeping her child alive—and now she was failing even to get pregnant again. She sobbed that she felt damaged and wanted to disappear—simply "slip out of life." Everything was too difficult, not worth the effort of getting through the day.

Bella wept through the entire session. While I had seen Bella cry tears of grief, I was witnessing the torrent of shame. She sobbed and sobbed, and I listened. As she left, I handed her a book off my shelf called *Healing Through the Dark Emotions,* by Miriam Greenspan. I marked the chapter where the author shares a personal story that speaks directly to Bella's situation.

Greenspan herself had a similarly tough decision to make when the prenatal group she had attended while pregnant was holding its postpartum get-together. Her son, Aaron, had lived for only sixty-six days, and had never left the hospital. "This would be a gathering of proud new moms and dads with their new two- and three-month-old babies," Greenspan wrote. "I got the invitation and cried."

Of course, there was no reason for her to go. She had no baby to hold in her arms. But when she imagined calling the new mom who was hosting the event to give her regrets, she felt frozen in grief. The thought of *not* going was as agonizing as the thought of going, so back and forth she went. What she really wanted to do was attend the event and bring a picture of Aaron. "It would be a way of saying, yes, I had this baby, and he was beautiful and he will always be my baby." She did not want to erase the fact of his life by not going. Then she immediately thought, no, she couldn't do this to a group of new parents. How could she bring death into such a joyous occasion?

In the end, Greenspan went because she knew that staying home would move her toward profound isolation.

I called and explained my predicament and was welcomed to the reunion. I showed my pictures of Aaron and spoke his name, described his personality and his spirit. I enjoyed, with a poignant ache, the newborn beauties that had just arrived on the planet. I left early, came home, and breathed a sigh of

**relief. I had not let my grief stop me, and this felt like a small triumph.**

Greenspan, herself an internationally known psychotherapist, shared this particular story to illustrate that we need not be stopped by grief from going where we want to go, doing what we need to do, or talking to whomever we need to talk to. Inspired by the author's example and her courage, Bella brought pictures of Anna to her high school reunion, giving herself permission to either show them or not, mention Anna or not, depending on how she felt at a particular moment. She did show the pictures of Anna to several people, and opened herself up to their loving and caring responses.

Attending the reunion allowed Bella to shed her shame like the false skin it was, and to reclaim her healthy anger. After the event she found out who was responsible for editing her daughter out of the newsletter. It turned out to be the sole act of the administrator she had spoken to on the phone, not a decision made by "consensus." She wrote him a formal letter of protest and sent copies to the school principal and the individual who chaired the reunion organizing committee. Taking such action on her own behalf felt to Bella like a large triumph—which it was.

## ROYAL ROADS TO COURAGE: HAPPINESS AND UNHAPPINESS

While others can help us remember our courage, we sometimes discover it entirely on our own. Our personal happiness and unhappiness can be royal roads to courage, if we are willing to stay open to our emotional experience.

## The Gift of Joy

Barbara, a therapy client of mine, stayed for years with a man addicted to drugs and alcohol. The marriage was riddled with fights, threats, and futile attempts to make her husband stay in treatment or maintain his sobriety. But Barbara never took a firm, bottom-line position until, as she tells it, she left a concert one evening with the certain knowledge that she was separating from Scott, and not reconciling, until he had gotten sober and was in ongoing treatment.

How did Barbara make the internal shift from complaining and blaming to this new, courageous place from which there was no turning back? As she spoke about the concert, which she described as beautiful and transcendent, it seemed that the music put her in touch with her own potentialities and capacity for joy, thus making her current painful situation suddenly, irrevocably intolerable. She discovered a profound truth: Whatever brings you joy and zest will enhance your ability to act bravely.

## The Gift of Unhappiness

Plain old unhappiness can also inspire us to make a courageous act of change. "There's buried treasure in unhappiness," says my writer friend Nancy Pickard, "and I've learned to mine it for all it's worth." Nancy had a good job in her twenties and was making good money, but she was unhappy. The job permitted her little creativity, which made her feel trapped and cheated. Allowing herself to fully feel her discontent, Nancy ultimately quit her job, gave up her apartment, and traveled with her boyfriend in Europe for three months. By the time she returned, she'd hatched a plan to try freelance writing rather than search for another corporate job. "It was unhappiness that got me there," she says. "I learned that unhappiness can give me courage, but in order to get that courage I have to be willing to let myself feel just as unhappy as I really am."

Seven years later, freelancing began to feel meaningless, and Nancy felt unhappy again. What she *really* wanted to do, she realized, was write fiction. She says, "I knew I could try to repress my discontent or I could surrender to it, which meant allowing myself to feel every ounce of unhappiness that I had, because that would fuel my next move." And so it did. She quit all her paying clients and starting working on fiction full-time. Now, twenty years later, she's a self-supporting novelist with seventeen published books to her name.

The moral of the story is not that if you're unhappy and quit your day job, you, too, will become a famous, best-selling author who loves her work. It's simply that you should be brave enough to acknowledge and honor your unhappiness, and if you can do this, your unhappiness will help you to be brave. As Nancy told me in a recent conversation, "I believe that when unhappiness arrives, courage is right around the corner. But if you don't let yourself admit to and feel the pain you're in, you will never get the gift of enough courage to do what you really want to do."

If you are one to ignore everyday unhappiness, not to worry. There are always abject misery and despair to remind you that you can no longer tolerate a particular job or relationship in its current form. Thank goodness for symptoms and suffering when they jolt us awake, bringing us back to ourselves and signaling the need for change. When the pain of the status quo is large enough, we may find the courage to inch forward or take a large leap, no matter how great our fear. And don't underestimate "inching." For every courageous change we make in our lives, the forward direction, not the speed of travel, is what really matters.

## WHO GIVES YOU COURAGE?

Throughout this book I've shared stories about women and men who have tapped into courage in the face of fear and shame. This is how we learn—through hearing the stories of others. We are naturally attracted by examples of courage because we want to know what it looks like and we want to know that we, too, can "do that."

We all need role models who inspire courage by sharing both their strength and their vulnerability. We inspire others by doing the same. When I was writing *The Mother Dance*, some of my colleagues who read the prepublication manuscript expressed concern about my generous sharing (as I saw it) of my honest experience and less-than-exemplary behavior. I made clear from the opening sentence that being a mother came as naturally to me as being an astronaut. I was warned by my colleagues that I would "lose credibility" as an expert in family relationships by sharing personal stories that vividly illustrated that when I get anxious or angry enough, I have the brain of a reptile.

But since *The Mother Dance* was published, readers, without exception, tell me that it is precisely this sharing of my vulnerability, limitations, and "Bad Mother Days" that helps them to gather the courage to stay ambulatory and breathing through each day. This isn't really so surprising. Who would want to read a parenting book written by a woman who sails effortlessly through motherhood, who is blissed out putting a snowsuit on a flailing toddler, or whose eyes always shine brightly when she says, "I am a mother," in response to the question, "What do you do?"

When I think about who in my own life has given me courage, I don't think about larger-than-life figures whose imperfections have been airbrushed out. I get courage to show up, to try, to act, to fail, to be my authentic, flawed, unique, ordinary self from my friends and role models, wherever I find them, who show me their own fully flawed humanity. I am neither drawn to, nor inspired by, folks who always seem to be competent and having a good day.

Actually, no one *gives* us courage—not experts, gurus, healers, artists, teachers, or heroes, fictional or real. The good people in our lives inspire us, push us, encourage us, cheer us on, advise us, support us, help us to strategize and figure out the first step, remind us of our own potentialities and possibilities. But rather than giving us courage, they help us to remember the courage we already have, and inspire us to act on it.

People *do* give us shame, and they may give generously both at the office and at home. Shame comes from the outside, although by the time we're adults we've internalized so much of it that even a tiny perceived insult from another can rev it up. Courage, in contrast, comes from the inside. It goes into hiding when we learn from experience that it is not safe to think, see, speak, and act authentically. If we are intentional about finding the places and people that inspire and empower us, we will remember that we can act courageously— a challenge that is at the heart of who we are in the world and what kind of world this is.

# Everyone Freaks Out

I once saw a brochure from one of our great national parks that said: "If you should find yourself in the jaws of a Grizzly Bear, remain calm. It can make the difference between your being badly mauled and losing your life." I knew immediately that this "how-to" tip wouldn't help me. I'm definitely not one to stay calm in such a situation, although I do take comfort in the notion that should I find myself in this very dilemma, I might be frozen stiff with terror. The bear, perhaps not being all that bright, might then think me calm or dead, or whatever it takes for a grizzly bear to suddenly lose interest, drop its dinner to the ground, and go off looking for new prey.

Nothing is more important than calming down, but it's not always possible. While we're on the subject of wildlife, here's another story that illustrates this point. Some years back I went to a two-week spiritual retreat in Arizona led by Carolyn Conger, a psychologist and one of the wisest people I've ever met. The experience included a solo retreat into the desert, where we would spend two days fasting and practicing total silence. In preparation we practiced several different meditations, the group energy allowing for a far deeper calm, stillness and centering than individuals might have achieved on their own. Afterward, we sat in a circle and each person told a story from his or her experience.

The story I remember best came from a woman who was more spiritually advanced than I could aim for. She had encountered a snake. Having practiced meditation with discipline for just this sort of eventuality before heading out on the retreat, she understood that no harm would come to her if she achieved the place of stillness and calm she knew was available to her. But there she was, face-to-face with a large rattlesnake, coiled, ready to strike, its rattling filling the otherwise silent desert air. All that she had practiced in the way of mindfulness and inner stillness was useless. She saw the snake and she freaked and froze—which was far more adaptive than trying to make a run for it.

The snake left her alone, but she was so disappointed in herself. She would have preferred to tell the group a different story, say a story of having looked death in the face and suddenly spotting a delicate blue flower growing out of a crack of rock and being filled with the beauty of the present moment. Or perhaps a story about experiencing a transcendent sense of "oneness" with the snake—a feeling of deep inner peace and resplendent joy at the recognition of their shared being-ness.

In fact, her story about the snake was just what the group needed—a reminder that we all freak out. Even in the absence of snakes and grizzly bears and other real threats, we can't rid ourselves of fear or always set it aside. The titles of countless self-help books on fear suggest otherwise, offering skills or techniques to *transcend* fear, *overcome* fear, *get beyond* fear, *triumph over* fear, live *without* fear, and so forth. Many of these books offer important and useful information. But forget about the notion that you can learn to triumph, transcend, and overcome at will. Sorry, not where fear and other discomfiting emotions are concerned. They will arrive uninvited for as long as you live—and they will also go.

Experts as divergent as mainstream mental health professionals and Eastern spiritual leaders teach that the best we can do with fear is to befriend it. That is, we can learn to expect, allow, and accept fear, observe it, watch it rise and fall, attend to how it feels in the body, watch it mindfully, and understand that fear will always reappear. Fear is a physiological process that cavorts and careens through our bodies and makes us miserable. Eventually it subsides   only, of course, to return. The real culprits are our knee-jerk responses to fear, and the ways we try to avoid fear, anxiety, and shame.

Don't get me wrong: Wanting to feel better fast is a perfectly natural human impulse. It's healthy to seek relief when you feel hopelessly mired in the emotional soup, and calming down is an essential first step to accurately perceiving a problem and deciding what to do about it. But the last thing you need to do is shut yourself off from fear and pain—either your own or the world's. If there is one overriding reason that our relationships and our world are in such a terrible mess, it's that we try to get rid of our anxiety, fear, and shame as fast as possible, regardless of the long-term consequences. In doing so, we blame and shame others, and, in countless ways, we unwittingly act at the expense of the self, the other, and the web of relationships we operate in. We confuse our fear-driven thoughts and behaviors (and those of our leaders) with what is right, best, necessary, or true.

When we think about fear, we tend to focus on a particular fear "of" something, such as planes, elevators, dating, illness, or failure. Far more daunting is the challenge of how to conduct ourselves in the dailyness of love and work when anxiety is chronically high and shame kicks in. This is the human condition. But, as we've seen, we needn't let anxiety and shame silence our authentic voices, close our hearts to the different voices of others, or stop us from acting with clarity, compassion, and courage. In today's world, no challenge is more important than that.

# Notes

## A Note on Professional Acknowledgments

The subject of this book is as large as life itself and lies at the heart of my work as a psychologist, psychotherapist, teacher, and writer. Fear and anxiety have been studied so comprehensively and exhaustively (shame, less so) that it's impossible, even with broad brush strokes, to track the origins of the ideas that are part of my current thinking or to credit the many pioneers in the field of human emotions. Suffice it to say that this book is the product of many people's ideas, although the responsibility for this work is mine alone.

That said, I do want to acknowledge the work of the late Murray Bowen and family systems theorists such as Dan Papero and Michael Kerr, who have studied how anxiety affects human behavior and organizational systems. For readers interested in learning more about "thinking systems" in the workplace, Jeffrey Miller's book, *The Anxious Organization*, is a key text.

Jerilyn Ross is one of many leading experts on anxiety disorders from a psychiatric and self-help perspective. In contrast to the voluminous literature aimed at helping individuals suffering from anxiety and stress, few books link the personal and political—an especially important challenge in today's fear-driven world. To this end I am grateful for Miriam Greenspan's book, *Healing Through the Dark Emotions: The Wisdom of Grief, Fear and Despair.* I'd put Greenspan's book on the global required-reading list, if I could.

No mention of names can begin to suggest the many people, including therapy clients, who have contributed over several decades to my understanding of human emotional functioning. My thanks to you all.

## Chapters 1 and 2    Why Can't a Person Be More Like a Cat/The Fear of Rejection

p. 8.          Rachel Naomi Remen on the difference between a "national" and individual diagnosis, "Top 5 Items to Grab When Evacuating a Hotel Room": Rachel Naomi Remen, quoted in "Holt Uncensored, #291, by Pat Holt, Tuesday, January 8, 2002. Also see Remen's book *Kitchen Table Wisdom* (New York: Riverhead Books, 1996).

p. 11.         Audre Lorde, *The Cancer Journals* (San Francisco: Spinster/Aunt Lute Books, 1980).

## Chapters 3 and 4    Terrified?/ In Praise of Anxiety

p. 27.         Airline ticket quotation from David Reynolds's book, *Even in Summer the Ice Doesn't Melt* (David K.

Reynolds, 1986), excerpted in *Yoga Journal,* May/June 1992.

p. 32.    Public-speaking story adapted from Harriet Lerner, "Speechless in Seattle," *Family Therapy Networker,* July/August, 2001. Also see "Public Freaking" by Barbara Ehrenreich, *Ms.,* September 1989.

## Chapter 5    The Trouble with Anxiety

p. 59.    "As author Susan Jeffers reminds us . . ." *Feel the Fear and Do It Anyway,* Susan Jeffers (New York. Ballantine Books, 1987).

p. 61.    Pat Love, *The Truth About Love* (New York: Fireside/ Simon & Schuster, 2001).

p. 65.    Overfunctioning and underfunctioning are key concepts in family systems theory, pioneered by the work of Murray Bowen.

## Chapter 6    Why We Fear Change

p. 73.    The story about Ben first appeared in my book, *The Dance of Intimacy* (New York: HarperPerennial: 1990).

p. 85.    Countermoves and "change back reactions" are an inherent part of the process of change as described by Murray Bowen. On coping with countermoves and changing entrenched patterns in stuck relationships, see my books *The Dance of Anger* (New York: HarperPerennial, 1986), and *The Dance of Intimacy.*

p. 86–88.     "My Mother/My Father/My Self" appeared in *Family Therapy Networker*, September/October 1984.

## Chapter 7    Your Anxious Workplace

Thanks to Katherine Kent for teaching me many of the ideas (based on Bowen family systems theory) that appear in this chapter, to Matt Lerner for sharing his wisdom about work relationships, and to Jeffrey Miller for writing *The Anxious Organization*.

p. 92.        Jeffrey Miller, *The Anxious Organization: Why Smart Companies Do Dumb Things* (Tempe, Ariz.: Facts on Demand Press, 2002).

## Chapters 8 and 9    The Secret Power of Shame/ The Fear of the Mirror

p. 129.       Adriana Gardella, "Living in the Shadow of a Lost Father," *Newsweek*, June 17, 2002.

pp. 144–146.  Natalie Kusz, "The Fat Lady Sings," in *The Bitch in the House*, Cathi Hanauer (New York: William Morrow, 2002).

pp. 162–170.  On the subject of the mislabeling of female genitals, my work has appeared in *New Woman* magazine, the *Journal of the American Psychoanalytic Association*, *The Dance of Deception*, the *Chicago Tribune*, and other publications.

## Chapter 10    When Things Fall Apart

Thanks to Ben Lerner for important conversation and wise editing on all chapters, especially this one.

p. 172.          Ian Frazier, "Researchers Say," *The New Yorker*, December 9, 2002

p. 176.          "Like a stain on our clothes." bell hooks, *All About Love: New Visions* (New York: William Morrow & Co., 2000).

                 "Between Living and Dying: A Conversation with Anne Finger About Abortion and Assisted Suicide." *Sun* (Chapel Hill, N.C.) 252, December 1996.

p. 177.          Michael Ventura, "A Primer on Death," in *Family Therapy Networker*, January/February 1996.

p. 191.          See Jon Kabat-Zinn, *Full Catastrophe Living* (New York: Delacorte Press, 1990), and *Wherever You Go There You Are* (New York: Hyperion, 1995).

p. 192.          Philip Simmons, *Learning to Fall: The Blessings of an Imperfect Life* (New York: Bantam Books, 2002).

p. 193.          Mary Pipher, *Letters to a Young Therapist* (New York: Basic Books, 2003).

## Chapter 11    Courage in the Face of Fear

pp. 215–216.     Miriam Greenspan, *Healing Through the Dark Emotions: The Wisdom of Grief, Fear, and Despair* (Boston: Shambhala Publisher, 2003).

# Index

Abandonment, fear of, 44, 180–81, by partner, 14, 21, 24, *see also* Rejection

Accommodating behavior, at work, 202–4, in marriage, 75–77

Acting "as if," 188–89, *see also* Pretending

Adoption reform movement, 137

Adventurous spirit, 197–98, desire to be, 202–4

Affirmations, 126–27, 179–80, 182, 189, 191, *see also* Inspirational messages; Positive thinking

Aftermath, of loss, 21–24, 128–32, of terrorist attacks, 7–8

Age shame, 135–36

*All About Love* (bell hooks), 229

American Psychiatric Association, diagnostic manual of, 51–52

Angelou, Maya, 136, 189

Anger, healthy vs. corrosive, 24, 124–25, 204–6, 213–16, letting go of, 21–26, *see* Blaming

Anxiety, 39–52, 53–72, about babysitter, 41–42, benefits of, 39–52, 94, as call to action, 40–43, and catastrophic thinking, 57–58, chronic, 223–4, contagiousness of, 97–104, deficiency of, 51–52, diagnosis of, 51–52, extremes of, 208–9, vs. fear, 11–13, and gut reactions, 43, 49, 53–54, and loss of perspective, 58–59, as mental disorder, 51–52, of mothers, 40–41, and negative effects on thinking and planning, 53–54, 58–60, 69–70, 190–95, in organizations, 92–116, persistence of, 43–47, physical effects of, 51–52, 55, 70, and polarized thinking, 75–77, and practicing tolerance for, 207–8, and serious outcomes, 6, as trickster, 54, 60, 70, underground, 57, 80–81, 94, 103–4, in the workplace, 13, 92–116

Anxiety disorders, types of, 52, 59–60

Anxiety-driven thinking, 56–58, 60–61, 69–70, 79–80, 93–97, 104–13, 221–24, *see also* Blaming; Negative thinking

*The Anxious Organization* (Jeffrey Miller), 92, 114
Anxious systems, 92–116
Appearance, anxiety and shame about, 13, 118, 141–70, overfocus on, 155–56, and self-perception, 157–58, *see also* Body shame
Apprehension, *see* Anxiety; Fear
Ault-Riché, Marianne, 107
Authenticity, 85, in relationships, 210–12, of voice, 224, as way of life, 202–4
Author's clients: Barbara, and bottom-line position with addicted husband, 217, Bella, and sharing daughter's death at high school reunion, 213–16, Craig and Janet, and cooking school story, 75–77, Elana, and "average" IQ, 137–40, Eliza, and social phobia after mother's death, 58–59, Frank, and escalator story, 14–20, Jane, and worry about low sex drive, 61–63, Jill, and fear "of everything," 207–8, Joan, and worry about husband's "platonic friendship," 43–47, Katy, and rubber band technique to stop negative thinking, 70–72, Louise, and confusing effects of mislabeling of female genitals, 162–64, Margot, as teenage survivor of suicide, 204–06, 212, Marion, and mother's "change back" reaction to her Ph.D., 79–85, Mary, and rejection by husband, 21–24, Mel, and shame about overweight son, 127–32, Paula, and shame about son who burned down building, 124–27, 132, Rhoda, and coping with chronic illness, 177–90, Sheila, as "super-sized chick," 146–55, Sonia, and distrust of psychiatrist, 48–49

Author's friends: Emily Kofron, on nightmarish quality of shame, 119, on mislabeling of female genitals, 166–67, Lena, on lesbian activism, 133–34, 137, Lorraine, on love for human body, 141–42, Marla (college year in India story), 197, Mary (home economics teacher's instructions on buying fabric story, 142–43, Nancy Pickard, on unhappiness as source of courage, 217–28, Sam (avoiding conflict at work story), 202–4
Author's stories: and anxiety-driven behaviors in workplace, 97–112, 200–2, as "Boney Maroney" adolescent, 143–44, and cosmic countermoves, 89–91, and fear of flying, 27–29, and fear of public speaking, 30–36, and fears about her children, 41–43, 56–57, 66, 219, with friends, 68, 109, in junior year of college in India, 197–98, with Outward Bound Program, 139, as overfunctioner, 66–68, 111–12, as overreactive, 41, 43, 56–57, 66, 109, and runaway underpants story, 119–20, as summer camp counselor, 158–59, when mother was diagnosed with cancer, 191–93, as unchosen, in fifth grade "slave sale," 122–23, as underfunctioner, 56–57, 66, 104–5, 97–112
Avoidance, of anxiety and fear, 6–7, 39, 206–7, as lifestyle (Jill), 207–8, of social situations, 29–30, 58–59

Barbara (friend and caretaker of Rhoda), 178–84, 190
Beck, Martha, 204
Berman, Jennifer, 11

Bipolar disorder, and suicide attempt (Margot), 204

Birth order, in workplace, 111–13, *see also* Sibling position

Blaming, 71–72, 95–97, 101–7, 125, 152, 179, 205, 223, *see also* Judgmentalness; Negative thinking

Body shame, 13, 118, 141–70, and mislabeling of female genitals, 161–70, *see also* Appearance; Shame

Bottom line, 115, 217, with critical husband, 210

Boundary violations, 103–4, 143, 148–55, 163–64

Calming down, 4, 8, 68 69, 71, 82, 107, 193, 221

Catastrophic thinking, 42, 57–59

Change, desire for, 15–21, fear of, 73 91

"Change back" reaction, 80–84, 88

Chronic illness (Rhoda), 177–90

Civil rights movement, 137

Conger, Carolyn, 221–22

Countermoves, 79–88, cosmic , 88 91

Courage, 194–195, 196–220, 199, to speak or act, 40, 83–84, 196, 204–6, 209–10, 212, 219 20, 224, of author, 196–98, 197–202, categories of, 210–12, and commitments, 211–12, definition of, 196–99, vs. fearlessness, 198, and happiness, 216–17, to let go, 21–24, to listen and question, 211, and role models for, 2–3, 129–30, 219–20, to exercise restraint, 40

Culture, shaming aspects of, 128–36, 143–44, 155, 174–77

"Dance," of over- and underfunctioners, pursuers and distancers, 65–66

Danger, denial of, 197–98, and fear, 53–54, responses to, 39–41

Death, fear of, coping with, 171–95, *see also* Illness

Depression, and chronic illness (Rhoda), 177–99, and suicide attempt (Margot), 204–6

Diagnoses, psychiatric, 51–52

Dieting for dollars story (Sheila), 146–55

Differences, anxiety about, 143–44, 160–61

Disability, 158–61, 176

Distance, in marital relationship, 21–22, 46–47

Distancing, 22, 66, 71–72, 97, 104, 107–9, to manage anxiety, 184–85, *see also* Fight-or Flight response

Divorce, 14, 21–24, 209

Dysfunctional bosses, 95–96

Dysfunctional family, 93

Dysfunctional organization, 92–116

Emotions, *see* Anxiety; Fear; Shame

Ensler, Eve, 166 68

Escalator story, 14–20

Evelyn, and chronically ill friend (Rhoda), 178, 181–85, 190

Failure, fear of, 77–78, benefits of, 18–21, 32–36

Family systems theory, 86–88, 89, 90, 116

Family triangle, author's, 86–91

Father-daughter relationship, 89 (author), 148–53 (Sheila), 163–64 (Louise)

Father loss, shame about, 128–32

Fear, of adventure and new learning and change, 6–7, 79–85, vs. anxiety, 11–13, 223, and avoidance, 6–7, as barrier to success in love and work, 9–10, benefits of, 5,

Fear (cont.)
10, 13, 36, 40, 49–51, 53, about children, 41–43, 197–98, and courage, 10–11, 22–24, 196–220, of death, 171–95, facing, 27–38, of failure, 6–7, 9, of female sexuality, 141–70, of flying, 27–29, of not being good enough, 128–32, 135–36, 141–70, 174–77, 203, of public speaking, 30–38, 117, 172, of rejection, 6–7, 14–26, and silence, 202–4, of success, 6–7, 9, 79–83, of terrorists, 7–8, see also Panic attacks; Phobias
Feel the Fear and Do It Anyway (Susan Jeffers), 180
Felix the cat, 1–3
Female genitals, anatomical variability in, 163, mislabeling of, 161–70, restoring pride in, 166–68
Female sexuality, 164–66, 168
Fight-or-flight response, 2, 39–40, 108
Finger, Anne, 176
Firstborns, 111–13
Frazier, Ian, 172
Freud, 166, 168
Friends, 66–68, as supporters in chronic illness, 178–90

Gardella, Adriana, 129–30
Gay, see Lesbianism
Gossip, 65, 97, 104, 109–11, 125–26
Grafton, Sue, 212
Greenspan, Miriam, 215–16
Grief, and chronic illness, 177–90, at death of child, 213–16, and fear, 173, healthy, 50, 121, lessons in, 171, and loss, 21, 130–31, and mustard seed story, 173, 175, 191, 195, being shamed for, 153, 176, 214–16

Healing Through the Dark Emotions (Miriam Greenspan), 215–16

Helplessness, 58, 115, 182
Honesty vs. blaming, 107
hooks, bell, 176
Humor, 11, 69, 71, 90–91, about aging, 136, about death, 172, 189–90, in face of chronic illness, 182, 189, as life raft in public speaking, 36–37, to lighten things up, 126–27

Illness, facing, 171–95
Inadequacies, feelings of, 25, 61–64, 131, see also Judgmentalness
Inferiority, see Inadequacies; Judgmentalness
Inspirational messages, 136–37
IQ tests and shame, 137–40

Jealousy, 43–47
Jeffers, Susan, 59, 180
Jordan, Judith, 119
Judgmentalness, 60–72, 124–27, 132, as anxiety–driven response, 60, 70, 82, 103, 106, and negative comparisons, 60–63, 69–70, 173–77, 190–91, see also Blaming; Negative thinking

Kabat–Zinn, Jon, 191
Karr, Mary, 93
Kusz, Natalie, 144–46

Lamott, Anne, 136
Laughter, see Humor
Learning to Fall (Philip Simmons), 192
Lesbianism, 133–34
Lesbian rights movement, 134, 137
Letters to a Young Therapist (Mary Pipher), 193–94
Lewis, Helen Block, 121
Limits, clarifying, 183–84, 211
Lindbergh, Anne Morrow, 173, 191
Living authentically, 1–3, 11, 13
Living mindfully, 194–95

Lorde, Audre, 11
Loss, 21–22, 77, of father, 128–33, of health, 171–75
Love, Pat, 61
Loyalties, unconscious, 78–79

Madanes, Cloe, 15
Male castration anxiety, and vulva, 168
Managing anxiety and fear, 96–97, 115, of death, 177–90, *see also* Blaming; Distancing; Gossip; Overfunctioning; Underfunctioning
Marriage, anxiety about poor prospects of, 155–58, fear of disrupting, 75–77, *see also* Status quo
Mason, Marilyn, 210
Meditation, 188, 193, 222
Men, and gender differences in handling shame, 212–13
Menninger Clinic, 111–12, 165, 200
Mentors, anxiety about disloyalty to, 78–79, and speaking up to, 204–6
Miller, Jeffrey, 92, 114
Mindful living, 194–95, 222
Mislabeling, of female genitals, 161–70
Mothering, and adult daughters, 79–83, and mother-blaming, 124–25, and shaming, 124–27, and guilt, 120–21, and learning to fear, 197–98
Motivation, to change, 15–21, 193–95
Mustard seed story, 173, 175, 191, 195

Negative thinking, 61–63, 68, 71, and illness, 179–90
Neurobiology, *see* Symptoms, physical
Night of a Thousand Screw--Ups, 34–35
Nin, Anaïs, 67

Obesity, *see* Overweight
Objectivity, loss of, 93–94
Obsessive thinking, 44, 52, 54, 68–69
Oldests, as overfunctioners, 104–5, 111–13
*Oprah Winfrey Show*, 130, 136
Organizational anxiety, 92–116, effects on superiors, 93–94, and loss of objectivity, 93–94, and stress, 196
Orgasm, 61–62
Overfocusing, 155, on appearance, 157–58, on actions of others, 67, 107
Overfunctioners, 65–66, 111–13, oldests as, 104–5, 111–13, *see also* Judgmentalness; Overfunctioning
Overfunctioning, 64–68, 72, of firstborn, 104–5, 111–13, and sibling position, 104–5, 111–13, under stress, 103, and unsolicited advice, 66, of youngests, 104–5, 111–13, *see also* Judgmentalness; Overfunctioners
Overfunctioning–underfunctioning dance, 99–102
Overweight, and shame, 144–55

Panic, 1, 29–30, 52, 55, 59, 70
Parenting, 41–43, 56–57, 124–127, 127–32, 197–98, 219–20, and secondhand shame, 124–32, *see also* Mothering
Patterned ways of moving under stress, 97, 103–13
Perfection, as trap, 35–36, 131
Personal growth, as threat, 75–77, 79–84
Phobias, 29–30, 52, 58–59, 123, *see also* Fears; Panic attacks; Symptoms, physical
Physical symptoms, *see* Symptoms
Pickard, Nancy, on unhappiness as source of courage, 217–18

Pipher, Mary, 193–94
Polarized relationships, and anxiety, 47, 75–77
Positive thinking, vs. negative thinking, 179–82, 187–88, *see also* Affirmations; Inspirational messages; Negative thinking; Pretending
Post-traumatic stress disorder, 52, 59
Pretending, to have answers, 38, power of, 127, 188–89, *see also* Acting "as if"
Psychotherapy, *see* Author's clients; Therapy
Public speaking, 30–38, 117, 172, and private speaking, 36–38
Pursuers, and distancers, 47, 66, *see also* Triangles

Rabelais, 168
Racism, 122–23, 135
Rationalization, of wrongdoers, 152–53
Reactivity, 10, 43, 60, 64, 67, 71, 82–83, 113, 115, 187, 198, and gossip, 111
Rejection, fear of, 14–26, and escalator story (Frank), 16–19, *see also* Abandonment; Shame
Remen, Rachel Naomi, 8
Resistance, 21, 85, 199, *see also* "Change-back" reaction; Countermoves; Reactivity
Reynolds, David, 27
Rich, Adrienne, 133
Rubber band technique, to stop negative thinking, 70–72
Ryun, Jim, 134

Safety, of sameness, 77
Scapegoating, *see* Blaming
Self-acceptance, 1–3, 155–58, 161
Self-appraisal, 49–50
Self-blame, *see* Judgmentalness

Self-consciousness, 58–59, 147, 143–44
Self-disclosure, 46–47, 131–32
Self-doubting, 64
Self-esteem, 21, 26, 53–72, 205
Self-help books, 4–5, 10–11, 222
Self-regulation, difficulties with, 152, 154–55
Self-righteousness, 64–66
Sensitivity, to criticism, 58–59
September 11 (9/11), 7–8
Setting limits, 72, 183–84
Sexual attraction, extramarital, 46–47
Sexual orientation, 133–134, 136
Sexual trauma, 163–64
Sexuality, 43, 61–63, 165–66
Shame, 4, 80, 117–40, 223–24, about aging, 135–36, and anger and aggression, 125, 213, about appearance, 13, 118, 141–70, and arrogance and avoidance, 11, at being rejected, 24–26, 122–23, and comparisons, 174–77, definition of, 118–21, and dependency and illness, 176–90, about differences, 128–32, 142–55, 160–61, vs. embarrassment, 119–20, at having no father, 128–32, about father loss, 128–132, gender differences in handling, 212–13, and grief, 176, 213–16, vs. guilt, 120–21, 124–25, 153, and secondhand shame, 123–138, and sexuality, 61–63, 161–70, and silence, 132–34, 202–4, about vulva, 162–70, about weight, 142–55, about who we are, 118–19, 121, 142–55
Shaming, 223–24, by doctors, 145–46, messages, 141–70, by mislabeling female genitalia, 162–64, packaged as help, 148, by parents, 148–55, of mothers, 125

Shyness, *see* Social phobia
Sibling position, 104–5, 111–13, *see also* Overfunctioning; Under-functioning
Sibling position, middle, 112–13
Silence, 109, 118, 134, costs of, 202–4
Simmons, Philip, 192
"Slave sale" story, 122–23
Social activism, 134, 137
Social phobia, 30, 52, 58–59, 123, 125–26
Societal norms, of beauty, 155–58
Speechless in Seattle, 30–32
Spirituality, 178–79, 193, 202–4, *see also* Affirmations
Stage fright, 30–38
Stephanie, at camp for disabled children, 159–61
Stereotypes, and age, 135–36
Status quo, fear of disrupting, 74–75, 79–85, 208–9
Steinem, Gloria, 136
Stigma, *see* Shame; Shaming
Stress, 5, 12, 58–59, 61–63, 65, *see also* Anxiety; Organizational anxiety, Organizations; Workplace
Success, fear of, 79–83
Suffering, human commonality of, 174–75, 208, 224
Suicide attempt (Margot), 204–6
Survival, in job, 115–16, after rejection, 14, 21–22, when things fall apart, 171–95, *see also* Illness
System, anxiety in, 85, 92–116, 134
Systems perspective, 96–97, 113–14
Symptoms, physical, of anxiety and fear and shame, 12, 29–32, 39–43, 48–49, 52, 54–55, 79–80, 118–19, 221–24

Therapist, 47–49, 93–194, 229, *see also* Author's clients

Therapy, 47–49, *see also* Author's clients
Triangles, 86–87, 95–96, 109–11
True, Shelley, 167–68

Underfunctioning, 64–67, 72, 104–5, 112–13
Underground anxiety, 57, 64, 67, 81, 93–94, 104
Underground tension, 108
Underreacting, 43, 150, vs. overreacting, 45–46
Unfairness of life, 171–95
Unhappiness and anxiety, as providing motivation for courage, 216–18

V Club, 169
*The Vagina Monologues* (Eve Ensler), 166–68, mislabeling of vagina, 161–70
Ventura, Michael, 177
Visibility, as shame buster, 108–9, 124–27, 132–33, 137–40, 204–6, 212, 213–16
Vulnerability, 51, 70, 147, 171, 195, of caregivers, 182–5, and shame, 177, courage to share, 219–20
Vulva, 162–70, as "complicated," 162–63, as threatening, 168, and "turkey wattles," confusion with vagina, 161–70

Weight, parental focus on, 127–32, 147–55
Women, and age shame, 135–36, and body shame, 141–70, facing illness, 171–95, and low sex drive, 61–63, and mislabeling of genitals, 161–170, and secondhand shame, 123–128, *see also* Culture, shaming aspects of
Women's movement, 137

Workplace, anxiety in, 92–116, and calming things down, 96, 102–3, 113, confusion with "family," 116, 202–4, scapegoating at work, 95–97, 107, 109, as system, 96–97, 113–14, underfunctioning in, 104–6
Worley, Jo-Lynne, 31–32

Worrying, obsessional, 52, *see also* Anxiety; Fear; Shame

Youngests, 104–5, as critical of authority, 105, and avoidance of leadership, 113, as overfunctioners, 111–13, as underfunctioners, 104–5, 112–13